jeet kune do basics

Jeet Kune Do

BASICS

David Cheng

TUTTLE PUBLISHING
Tokyo • Rutland, Vermont • Singapore

Published by Tuttle Publishing, an imprint of Periplus Editions (HK) Ltd., with editorial offices at
364 Innovation Drive, North Clarendon, Vermont 05759 U.S.A.

Library of Congress Cataloging-in-Publication Data

Cheng, David, 1959-
  Jeet Kune Do basics / David Cheng.—1st ed.
    191 p. : ill.; 25 cm
  Includes bibliographical references.
  ISBN 0-8048-3542-X (pbk.)
  1. Jeet Kune Do. I. Title. GV1114.6.C537 2003
  796.815--dc22

                         2003027961

ISBN-10: 0-8048-3542-X
ISBN-13: 978-0-8048-3542-8

Distributed by

North America, Latin America & Europe
Tuttle Publishing
364 Innovation Drive
North Clarendon, VT 05759-9436 U.S.A.
Tel: 1 (802) 773-8930
Fax: 1 (802) 773-6993
info@tuttlepublishing.com
www.tuttlepublishing.com

Asia Pacific
Berkeley Books Pte. Ltd.
130 Joo Seng Road #06-01
Singapore 368357
Tel: (65) 6280-1330
Fax: (65) 6280-6290
inquiries@periplus.com.sg
www.periplus.com

Japan
Tuttle Publishing
Yaekari Building, 3rd Floor
5-4-12 Osaki
Shinagawa-ku
Tokyo 141 0032
Tel: (81) 3 5437-0171
Fax: (81) 3 5437-0755
tuttle-sales@gol.com

First edition
10 09 08 07   10 9 8 7 6 5 4 3
Printed in Singapore

TUTTLE PUBLISHING ® is a registered trademark of Tuttle Publishing, a division of Periplus Editions (HK) Ltd

table of contents

DEDICATION

This book is dedicated first, to God the Father,
the Lord Jesus Christ, and the Holy Spirit, who together are
the source of inspiration and guidance in my life.

And second, to my wife, Vera, and my children,
Lauren and Jonathan, who have supported me and been patient
with me as I worked on the book. Much love to you all.

acknowledgments

I WOULD LIKE TO THANK Chris Kent, my teacher, mentor, and friend, for his invaluable instruction in the art of Jeet Kune Do over the years and for opening my eyes to my potential, using Bruce Lee's art as a vehicle.

I would also like to express my thanks to various original students of Bruce Lee who have illuminated my understanding of Jeet Kune Do, namely, Bob Bremer, Richard Bustillo, Dan Inosanto, Pete Jacobs, Taky Kimura, Daniel Lee, Jerry Poteet, Patrick Strong, and Ted Wong. Thanks to second-generation instructors Cass Magda, Tim Tackett, and Dan Sullivan, who have also helped me in my journey.

Thanks also to Jeff Scharlin—my good friend, training partner, Jeet Kune Do brother, and a solid teacher in his own right—for his friendship, suggestions, and assistance in this project. His feedback and criticisms were very helpful.

I would also like to thank Jaimee Itagaki, photographer extraordinaire, for her keen eye and invaluable suggestions in taking the pictures for this book. Her professionalism and easy-going personality helped make the work so enjoyable.

Much appreciation goes to my students who assisted in the photographs for the book, namely, Andrew Kim, Luca Levorato, Jeff Ng, Moamer Qazafi, and Stanley Quon. Thanks also to my other students, who have contributed to my own growth. They are all helping to keep the Jeet Kune Do legacy alive.

Book participants (left to right): Luca Levorato, Moamer Qazafi, David Cheng, Jeff Scharlin, Andrew Kim, Jeff Ng (not pictured—Stanley Quon)

introduction

THERE IS A JOKE that says, "If you ask ten different Jeet Kune Do instructors what Jeet Kune Do is, you will get ten different answers." Another joke in the same vein asks, "How many Jeet Kune Do instructors does it take to screw in a light bulb?" Answer: "Five—one to screw in the light bulb, and four to tell him that he's doing it wrong."

What these bits of humor tell us is that there is wide disagreement about the nature of Jeet Kune Do. Some believe that it is basically a system with certain techniques and principles. Others think it is a philosophy, an approach to martial arts that helps each person develop his or her own style of fighting. As with many things, each interpretation has some truth to it.

However, to truly understand Jeet Kune Do, we must examine its roots; we must observe where it has been, as well as where it is today. In these beginning chapters, we will look at how Jeet Kune Do originated and developed. To assist us in our understanding, we will also examine the basic principles that constitute the framework of the art. Finally, we will consider the state of Jeet Kune Do today, in terms of some of the most prominent interpretations. Having this background will give us a good start in appreciating the different elements that make up Jeet Kune Do.

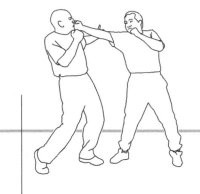

history and development of jeet kune do

ALTHOUGH JEET KUNE DO is a young martial art, it generates more interest than many of its older counterparts. This is due, in large part, to the enigmatic life of its founder, Bruce Lee. We can safely say that Lee is so intertwined with the art that one cannot think of Jeet Kune Do without thinking of Bruce Lee. Therefore, to understand the history and development of Jeet Kune Do, we must examine the evolution of Lee himself as a martial artist.

Lee was born on November 27, 1940, in San Francisco, California. The following year, his family moved to the cramped, tropical environment of Hong Kong where he spent his childhood and teenage years growing up. Early on, Lee was exposed to taijiquan, an art practiced by his father. He also studied a little bit of Hung Gar, a southern style of gung fu (or kungfu). However, his primary formal gung fu training did not begin until his early teens, when he began learning Wing Chun, a close-quarters fighting style that emphasizes hand-trapping techniques. He studied for several years under the supervision of Yip Man, the head instructor of Wing Chun at his school.

Lee was obsessed with Wing Chun and practiced frequently. While other students were content to learn the art as a sport, Lee was interested in learning how to fight. He and other students engaged in several sparring matches with people from outside the school, quickly gaining a formidable reputation. This emphasis on practical, street-oriented testing would later play a major role in the creation of Jeet Kune Do.

During this time, Lee examined other gung fu styles. He also practiced dancing and became the cha-cha champion of Hong Kong. The knowledge that he gained from these experiences served as a reservoir of material when he developed his approach to martial arts.

At age eighteen Lee reached a turning point in his life. A rather poor student, he had little prospect of acceptance into college. Also, when he injured someone during a street fight, the parents of the victim lodged a complaint with the local police. Lee's parents, worried about his future, literally shipped him off to the United States so that he could be away from the violent environment and also reclaim his American citizenship. So, in 1959 Lee returned to the place of his birth, San Francisco. After a short stay he relocated to Seattle, Washington, where he enrolled in the Edison Technical School and worked at a local restaurant owned by a family friend.

While attending high school, Lee continued to practice Wing Chun. Jesse Glover, a fellow student at Edison, used to watch Lee as he executed his techniques. Suitably impressed, Glover decided to make friends with the young man so he could learn from him. Lee began to share some of his knowledge with Glover. Glover introduced other friends to Lee, and it was not long before Lee had gathered a small group of followers, eager to learn this little-known and intriguing art. With no *kwoon* (school, or training place) readily available, Lee taught his students wherever there was space, including parking lots and outdoor parks.

At first, Lee faithfully taught Wing Chun as he had learned it. However, as he worked out with different students, he discovered that some of the classical techniques did not work as well in his new circumstances, particularly against the larger American students. This situation compelled Lee to make modifications to his techniques. The changes he made were extensive enough that he no longer felt comfortable calling his art "Wing Chun." Instead, he eventually renamed it *Jun Fan*, using his own Cantonese name.

When Bruce Lee first developed Jeet Kune Do, he saw it as primarily a combination of Wing Chun, fencing, and boxing. He also considered it a Chinese gung fu system, but without branches, formality, and tradition.

Lee graduated from Edison Technical School and enrolled at the University of Washington, where he majored in philosophy. He was deeply fascinated with Chinese philosophy, especially as it related to gung fu. Some of Lee's students—now including Taky Kimura, who later became his best friend and

Defining Jeet Kune Do

"**W**hat is Jeet Kune Do (JKD)? Chinese martial art, definitely! It is a kind of Chinese martial art that does away with the distinction of branches, an art that rejects formality, and an art that is liberated from the tradition." (Lee 1997, p. 47)

assistant instructor—encouraged him to start a school and to charge for lessons, so that he would not have to continue doing menial work. As a result, Lee established what would be the first Jun Fan Gung Fu Institute at the University of Washington, where he taught his modified form of Wing Chun.

In 1964, after getting married, Lee and his new bride moved to Oakland, California, to live with James Lee, an active gung fu practitioner whom he had met several years earlier. Over the years Lee and James developed a strong friendship. James became fascinated with Lee's incredible speed and power, and endeavored to learn his system of gung fu. At the same time Lee was impressed with James's accomplishments in weight training, and James introduced him to many of the concepts that Lee later incorporated into his own development. Together, Lee and James decided to establish a second Jun Fan Gung Fu Institute in Oakland. Admission to the Institute was highly selective, and only the most serious candidates were allowed to train in Jun Fan.

Some members of the gung fu community in nearby San Francisco became aware that Lee was teaching non-Chinese students. Both Lee and James disagreed with the traditional idea of teaching gung fu only to persons of Chinese descent, and this upset the traditionalists. They sent a newly arrived Chinese gung fu teacher to Lee's school to present an ultimatum: either stop teaching non-Chinese or fight the teacher.

Not one to back off, Lee refused to budge on the issue of teaching non-Chinese, and he accepted the challenge. At first, the representative and his entourage wanted to set up rules, such as no hits to the groin. However, Lee insisted on having no restrictions. The fight occurred behind closed doors. Lee adhered primarily to his modified Wing Chun style during the confrontation, which he eventually won by chasing the challenger all over the room, then keeping him subdued until he gave up.

While there is some dispute as to how long the fight lasted, there is no question that Lee was unhappy with his performance. Even though he won the fight, he felt tired and winded. Lee also found that the close-range fighting techniques of his modified Wing Chun were too limiting, because they did not allow him to end a fight quickly, particularly when his opponent fled from him. Lee realized that he needed to greatly improve his conditioning and that he needed to include other weapons in his art, to deal with opponents when they were farther away.

As a result, Lee started to incorporate more aerobic training, such as running, into his personal program, to strengthen his conditioning. Also, he added intermediate-range kicks from French *Savate* and Northern gung fu, as well as medium-range punches from Western boxing. He modified the stance so that his strong side, the right lead, was placed forward. Moreover, he made the stance more mobile by incorporating boxing- and fencing-style footwork. While Lee kept some of the trapping techniques and principles that he inherited from Wing Chun, he discarded others. In order to be incorporated into his approach, a particular technique, whatever its source, had to fit in with the other techniques and represent an efficient way of accomplishing its purpose.

In his research into ultimate combat, Lee also realized that it was best not to defend passively. He concluded that striking as an opponent prepared to attack represented a more efficient and effective way to defend. This idea of intercepting one's opponent became the most significant change in Lee's thinking during this time.

In the latter part of his life, Lee's ideas on combat and martial arts training proved to be controversial. Many traditional martial artists felt upset and offended at some of his pronouncements. Over time, however, many martial artists have accepted his ideas.

In 1966 Lee and his family moved to Los Angeles after he signed a contract to appear in a television series that never got off the ground. While on retainer to the studio, Lee had freedom to continue researching and training in martial arts. He spent time teaching Dan Inosanto, a *Kempo* black belt, who had studied with him ever since he served as Lee's escort a few years earlier, when Lee gave a demonstration at Ed Parker's Long Beach International Tournament. During a discussion with Inosanto about his approach to combat, Lee came up with a new name, "Jeet Kune Do"—"the way of the intercepting fist"—which he thought best characterized the essence of his art at this time.

After Lee had been teaching Inosanto and a couple of others for a while in the back of a pharmacy in Chinatown, Lee and Inosanto launched the third Jun Fan Gung Fu Institute, in February 1967, in a nondescript building in the nearby area. Inosanto became Lee's assistant instructor at the Institute. Lee himself taught at the school, and in addition, he took on private students, some recruited from the school. These private sessions gave Lee a chance to experiment with new ideas that he researched, with his students acting as willing guinea pigs. Lee also began to study grappling and wrestling with some of the best practitioners of the day.

As the 1960s drew to a close, Lee's skill in speed, power, and closing in on an opponent increased so much that no one could stop him, even when he told opponents what he intended to do. Because no one could stop his strikes, he found it unnecessary to use his trapping skills, although trapping continued to be part of the curriculum at all three Institutes. In 1970, while recuperating from a back injury, Lee recorded many notes and observations on combat, and on Jeet Kune Do in particular. That same year, Lee decided to close all three of his Jun Fan Gung Fu Institutes because he was concerned that it was too easy for a member to take the agenda as "the truth" and the schedule as "the way."

In 1971, dissatisfied with the lack of progress in his acting career in the United States, Lee traveled to Hong Kong in hopes of establishing himself as a martial arts film star. Also, he believed that the best way to showcase his combative philosophy to a wide audience was through motion pictures.

His own thinking about martial arts continued to evolve as well. He saw that interception, while important, was not necessarily the answer for all situations or for all students. Lee began to look at Jeet Kune Do as the "way of no way," in which a martial artist was not bound by any particular style or method, but could use all ways and all methods to adapt to any kind of opponent.

Nowhere was this view more graphically displayed than in the fighting scenes he managed to film for the unfinished movie *Game of Death*. In that film Lee had to fight a Filipino Escrima master, a Hapkido stylist, and a seven-foot freestyle fighter in the form of Kareem Abdul-Jabbar. He had to adapt his own fighting methods and tactics to deal with the particular challenges presented by each opponent. Lee showed how one must be proficient in all ranges of combat and with all kinds of tools. The few sequences that he filmed showed a martial artist who was equally adept at kicking, punching, trapping, grappling, and weaponry. This was perhaps the highest evolution of Jeet Kune

Lee was against what he called the "classical mess" practiced by other martial artists because he believed that what were once fluid, realistic movements had settled into mechanical routines. He wanted martial artists to return to the original ideal of freedom in fighting.

Do that Lee achieved before his untimely death in July 1973.

When Lee passed away, the world lost one of the century's greatest martial artists. Moreover, some thought, and still believe, that his art of Jeet Kune Do died with him. Although undoubtedly Lee took some of what he knew with him to the grave, much of what is now regarded as Jeet Kune Do has, fortunately, been preserved through a combination of several sources. Lee's surviving assistant instructors, Taky Kimura and Dan Inosanto, continue to pass on the knowledge that Lee gave them. Other first-generation and later students are also active, to different degrees, in propagating Lee's art as they learned it. Lee's notes, in which he documented many of his thoughts about combat, also provide important knowledge about Jeet Kune Do. Finally, Lee's martial arts films show different aspects of his fighting philosophy in action, providing further insight into his art. The compilation of this knowledge will allow future generations to learn about, and to perpetuate, Jeet Kune Do.

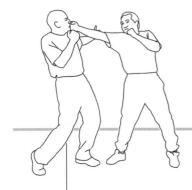

chapter 2
philosophy and
guiding principles

JEET KUNE DO contains a definite structure and specific principles that have guided its development. As Lee examined different martial arts, he used these principles to evaluate whether or not a particular technique should be included in the art. A technique had to fit into the existing structure and work efficiently with other techniques in order to be included.

The maxim "Absorb what is useful, reject what is useless, and add what is specifically your own," characterizes the "research" and "experimental" aspects of Jeet Kune Do. In his research Lee tried to identify techniques that could enhance his fighting style and to understand how other stylists fought so that he could develop ways to counter them. He critically read thousands of books on judo, boxing, wrestling, fencing, and other arts, often underlining the text and making notes in the margins when a particular idea struck him as significant. Lee also attended demonstrations and martial arts tournaments, carefully watching participants in order to understand the essence of their style. He sought out and trained with martial artists from many disciplines so that he could learn from them.

Lee concluded that kata, or forms, had limited usefulness because they bore little resemblance to real combat. Recognizing that fights did not fall into established patterns, he regarded these exercises as "swimming on dry land." Lee believed that to become an effective fighter, one had to actually swim in the water, which meant sparring.

JKD Philosophy in the Movies

Watch Bruce Lee's films carefully, and you can catch bits of his martial arts principles. In *Enter the Dragon*, he explains to the senior abbot that it is not he who hits, but that "it" hits all by itself. This is an example of the principle of nonintention.

Lee also came to understand that, in order to adapt to the changing dynamics of a real fight, a person had to develop skill in combat at any range. He realized, for example, that Wing Chun worked best at close range, but that other methods were needed, for both close range and other distances. Therefore, Lee incorporated kicking techniques from other gung fu systems, as well as Savate, for intermediate-range fighting. He also took punching techniques from Western boxing for intermediate range. Finally, he added chokes, strangleholds, locks, throws, and takedowns for close range.

Lee concluded that it was important to aggressively close in on an opponent, rather than passively wait for an opponent to approach. Further, it was better to avoid being hit than to block an attack. Thus, Lee drew on fencing and Western boxing because their superior footwork and mobility allowed him to quickly bridge the gap when attacking and to quickly evade when being attacked.

Many of the principles of Jeet Kune Do were borrowed from Western fencing. These include broken rhythm, interception, and simple and direct movements. Indeed, Lee's art has been characterized as "fencing without a foil."

Many martial arts systems that Lee examined were of the "block and hit" variety. When a person was attacked, that person would block the strike and follow up with a strike. Through fencing, Lee found a more efficient way to deal with an attack. A good fencer would not merely block or parry an attack but would strike as an opponent prepared to attack, thus intercepting the attack. Lee applied this principle to empty-handed fighting, meaning that a person could intercept with a punch or kick as the opponent started to attack.

Lee realized that no single martial arts system had all the answers to every situation. Thus, to stick to one particular "way" of fighting, as he called it, was to cling to "partiality." Rather than be bound to any particular style, Lee strove for "totality" in fighting, using any method that worked, no matter what its source. He believed that individuals should train their "tools" (the parts of the body used for fighting) for maximum effectiveness, according to their own abilities, and that this training was more important than any style. Individuals should experience "freedom of expression" in fighting, so that they can act in response to reality, rather than to a preconceived notion of what a fight "should" be like.

Lee's extensive research led to the following principles, which guided the development of his art:

- Simple, Direct, and Economical: Techniques should not be overly complicated, but should go directly to the intended target with a minimum of movement. A strike along a straight line, rather than a wide curved path, is more efficient.

- Nontelegraphic Movement: One should not show any unnecessary preparatory movement that would alert an opponent as to what one is about to do.

- Nonclassical: No set or fixed forms or patterns are utilized, because they do not represent actual fight situations.

> Generally speaking, Lee did not see value in the practice of gung fu forms and karate katas, because they did not match actual fighting situations. The exceptions were the *sil lum tao* from Wing Chun and a kicking set that he had developed.

- Strong Side Forward: The strongest weapons should be placed in front, facing the opponent, where they can reach the target faster and do the most damage. The weaker weapons are placed at the rear, where they become stronger because they have to travel a farther distance to the target.

- Hand before Foot: When one is executing hand strikes, the hand should strike the target slightly before the lead foot lands. In this way one's body weight is behind the strike.

- Centerline: A principle carried over from Wing Chun, maintaining the centerline enables one to control an opponent's balance, position, leverage, and ability to attack. Strikes down the centerline are difficult for the opponent to see and to defend against.

- No Passive Moves: Rather than merely block or parry a strike, one should either combine defensive moves with offensive moves or defend by counterattacking.

- Longest Weapon to the Nearest Target: In attacking, one should employ the weapon with the longest reach against the closest target presented by the opponent. This allows one to strike the opponent as quickly as possible.
- Adaptability: Because the dynamics of a fight constantly change, one must quickly change to respond appropriately. A fighter must not be bound by fixed techniques or patterns, but use whatever works, without limitation.
- Broken Rhythm: Disrupting the rhythm of an opponent allows one to catch an opponent short while he is engrossed in his own tempo, making it harder for him or her to defend or counter.
- Water in the Hose. This term describes the idea of maximizing the power of strikes by training with them until they are like water bursting through a fire hose when they hit the target.
- Whip: By striking with a punch or kick and then recoiling like the action of a whip, one can retract the striking limb quickly. This action is combined with the "water in the hose" principle so that power and speed can be maximized.
- Short Arc Principle: After a punch hits, the hand should move in a small arc as it returns to its ready position. In that way it goes in a continuous path from beginning to end without stopping, which brings the hand back rapidly.
- Nonintention: One should strike without thinking or conscious decision. Thinking about hitting slows down a fighter's reaction. Instead, it should be as if the limb strikes by itself, without thought.
- Simultaneous Parry and Hit: Instead of blocking a strike and then returning a strike, it is more efficient to parry and hit at the same time.
- Hammer: By lowering one's lead hand slightly at the elbow, with a motion like a hammer's, one can subtly gain distance on an opponent. This enables one to strike from a closer distance to reach the target more quickly.

> My instructor, Chris Kent, used to describe Jeet Kune Do as a "principled martial art." The principles explained why certain things were done. The techniques represented the expressions of the principles. Both were an integral part of the overall art.

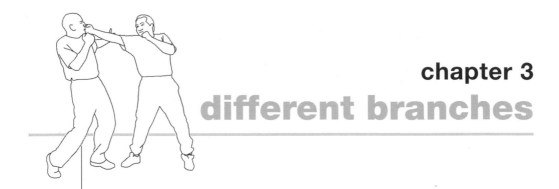

chapter 3
different branches

I is easy to be confused about what constitutes Jeet Kune Do because people view the art in different ways. When Bruce Lee was still alive, relatively few people trained in the art and Lee could exercise control over what was taught. Since his passing, different interpretations of Jeet Kune Do have arisen. This has occurred because Jeet Kune Do itself is somewhat open-ended, with no fixed number of techniques and, in most cases, no set curriculum. In addition, Jeet Kune Do encourages individual freedom of expression, such that different instructors emphasize different aspects.

As a result, different camps have emerged, each claiming to follow the true path laid down by Lee. These range from individuals who believe strongly in preserving Jeet Kune Do just as it was practiced when Lee was alive, to those who believe in Jeet Kune Do as primarily a framework for formulating an individualized approach to fighting. The following is an overview of the major interpretations.

Jun Fan/Modified Wing Chun

Individuals in this category practice techniques and methods that Lee embraced during his early years in the United States. They consist primarily of the modified Wing Chun trapping that Lee taught at that time. Some practitioners faithfully preserve Lee's teachings. Others have modified the art, bringing their own distinctiveness to it. Strictly speaking, this art is pre-Jeet Kune Do. Some believe that it is actually more practical and combative than Jeet Kune Do. These methods were taught and developed at the Seattle Jun Fan Gung Fu Institute. Hence, they are regarded as arising during the "Seattle Era."

Original Jeet Kune Do

These practitioners emphasize the art as taught and practiced by Lee from the mid-1960s to 1973. This interpretation consists of some of the Jun Fan trapping methods from the earlier period and the fencing, kickboxing, Western boxing, and grappling influences that were later added. Original Jeet Kune Do was taught at the Oakland Jun Fan Gung Fu Institute and the Los Angeles Chinatown Jun Fan Gung Fu Institute. Hence, the art, as taught during this time, is known as the "Oakland Era" and "Chinatown Era."

The strongest push for perpetuating this interpretation of Jeet Kune Do came from the Bruce Lee Educational Foundation during the 1990s. This organization was composed of Lee's widow and daughter; first-generation students of Lee from the Seattle, Oakland, and Los Angeles eras; and a few second-generation students. The efforts of these individuals exposed more people to Lee's art, as it existed during his lifetime.

Proponents of this interpretation are often accused of remaining stuck in the past and refusing to change with the times. However, they view the original art as remaining effective because principles such as directness, economy of motion, and interception remain just as valid today as they were back then. They believe that, rather than adding to Lee's art, as many seemingly have done, practitioners should concentrate on refining their techniques and improving their skills.

Origin of the Term "Concepts"

Because he promised Bruce Lee that he would never commercialize his art, at seminars Dan Inosanto would tell participants that he could not teach Jeet Kune Do but would show them concepts from the art. Savvy promoters began to advertise that Inosanto would teach "Jeet Kune Do Concepts."

Jeet Kune Do Concepts

These practitioners view Jeet Kune Do not as a system or style, but rather as a philosophical approach towards developing a personal expression of fighting. Although they regard Lee's original art as a starting place, they believe that a student should evolve from there. Just as Lee researched many arts during his lifetime, Concepts proponents encourage martial artists to examine different styles to add those elements that work best for them.

Hence, Concepts practitioners will often study, in addition to Lee's original art, Filipino martial arts, Muay Thai, shoot wrestling, Silat, and Brazilian jujitsu. They stress Lee's philosophical approach to martial arts, rather than specific techniques and training methods, as the true spirit of Jeet Kune Do.

"My purpose in creating Jeet Kune Do was not to compare with other branches of martial arts. Anything that becomes a branch would induce bad feeling. Once there is a formation of a branch, then things seem to stop. Students would labor for regulations and rules. Then the meaning of martial art would be lost." (Lee 1997, p. 327)

Some think that Concepts practitioners have watered down Lee's art by adding other arts. They believe that some of Jeet Kune Do's principles, such as simplicity, strong side forward, and directness, have been compromised as influences from other arts have crept in. Concepts students respond that Lee's original art can be preserved but that Jeet Kune Do is a highly individualized process to explore one's own freedom of expression.

Is JKD a Style or a Philosophy?

Although some think it is one or the other, it really is both. Jeet Kune Do is not a fixed style, but it does have certain structures and techniques that give it a certain look. It also contains philosophical elements that provide reasons for its structures and techniques.

Functional Jeet Kune Do

More recently, some are pushing the definition of Jeet Kune Do even further. Calling their approach "Functional Jeet Kune Do," they seek to recapture the notion of training and fighting with "aliveness." Dissatisfied with what they regard as "dead pattern" drills taught by many Jeet Kune Do instructors, they emphasize constant training against moving and resisting partners rather than passive recipients.

The proponents of this approach do not carry on most of Lee's original art. Indeed, they regard trapping techniques to be virtually useless against modern-day fighters. Instead of the kicking, punching, trapping, and grappling methods that are part of many Jeet Kune Do curricula, Functional Jeet Kune Do practitioners train in Western boxing, Thai boxing, Greco-Roman wrestling, and Brazilian jujitsu. They believe that these training methods help students to become competent fighters more quickly than traditional approaches to Jeet Kune Do. As a result, they probably have more in common with students of mixed martial arts than with other Jeet Kune Do students.

There are undoubtedly practitioners who hold other interpretations of Jeet Kune Do, but these are the more prominent approaches practiced today. Proponents of each interpretation sincerely believe that they are following the path that Lee laid down.

The emergence of different, often contradictory, interpretations of Jeet Kune Do may be unfortunate, but not surprising. It parallels what has occurred in other martial arts, such as Wing Chun and Filipino Kali, Escrima, and Arnis. A divergence of views often happens after the founder of an art passes away.

Jeet Kune Do, by definition, allows practitioners to evolve their own expression of fighting. However, it remains important to preserve and promote the art as Lee researched, practiced, and taught it, so that future generations can benefit from the knowledge and training that he developed.

part 2
getting started

I T TAKES A SIGNIFICANT COMMITMENT of time, energy, and usually money to study a martial art such as Jeet Kune Do. Although you can potentially learn useful self-defense skills in a short period of time, in order to gain proficiency in the art as a whole, you must be willing to make an investment of your resources. Hence, rather than dive in blindly, it makes sense for someone who is thinking about Jeet Kune Do to understand what to expect in a teacher and in his or her training.

In the next few chapters, we will take a look at how a prospective student can go about selecting an appropriate school or teacher. The task is not as simple as looking up a training facility in the phone book. We will also examine what a typical Jeet Kune Do class is like and what to expect during the first few months of training. Finally, the important topic of safety in training will be considered. Having this background will make it easier for you to make an informed and intelligent decision about training in Jeet Kune Do.

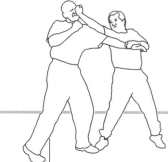

chapter 4
choosing the right
school or teacher

STUDENTS WHO WANT TO STUDY Jeet Kune Do will learn best by training directly with a knowledgeable instructor. The challenge for many prospective students is to find such a person. While it is relatively easy to locate a school that teaches a traditional art, such as karate or taekwondo, there are not many Jeet Kune Do teachers around. The majority of those who teach some form of Jeet Kune Do reside in the United States and Europe, so individuals who live in other countries will have a difficult time finding an instructor.

Learning from Videotapes and Books

Students who live too far from a Jeet Kune Do teacher can still learn, to some extent, by watching a Jeet Kune Do videotape or reading a Jeet Kune Do book. There are a number of excellent videotapes and books available that feature top-notch instructors. The Resources section at the end of the book lists some of these videotapes and books.

To complicate matters, many of those who instruct in Jeet Kune Do do not publicize that fact. They maintain a low profile, quietly teaching small groups of students in garages and backyards. One usually hears about them only through word of mouth. So, while you can easily pinpoint a school that offers traditional martial arts training in the telephone book, you are not likely to come across a Jeet Kune Do instructor that way.

Someone looking for a local school that teaches a traditional art can easily identify a large organization or association that governs that style. These groups can refer individuals who are interested in learning their art to member schools in their area. However, there is no wide-ranging group that oversees the various Jeet Kune Do schools and instructors that a prospective student can contact.

Given these difficulties, you must possess a strong commitment to learning Jeet Kune Do in order to find the right school or instructor. So how can you find out who is teaching, and where? One place to start is the Internet. A number of Jeet Kune Do teachers and schools have Web sites that can be accessed easily through the various search engines. Another source is Web sites devoted to the subject of Jeet Kune Do or Bruce Lee. These sometimes have links to various Jeet Kune Do schools.

> **Seminar Training**
>
> Many Jeet Kune Do instructors travel to different cities to give seminars. This is an excellent way for students with no access to a local school to obtain periodic training. While in town, the seminar instructor may be available for private lessons as well.

Some well-known Jeet Kune Do instructors have their own associations and students who are authorized to teach. They maintain lists and contact information for these students as part of their own Web sites. There are also other individuals who, as a service to prospective students, keep lists of Jeet Kune Do instructors as part of their Web sites.

Another way that a prospective student can use the Internet to find a Jeet Kune Do instructor is to post a message on a Jeet Kune Do discussion forum. Because these forums attract a large number of people from all over the world, there is a good chance that someone will know of a Jeet Kune Do instructor in a certain area.

A few Jeet Kune Do instructors and schools advertise in martial arts magazines, so it is worth the effort to check out those publications. Also, martial arts supply stores will sometimes have brochures or flyers advertising the services of a local Jeet Kune Do teacher.

Even after you have found a Jeet Kune Do instructor, you must evaluate whether that instructor offers what you want to learn. Because of the myriad of interpretations of Jeet Kune Do, what a particular Jeet Kune Do instructor teaches may or may not be what you want to learn. Different instructors vary significantly in terms of the material that they teach. Some teachers offer training in the curriculum that Lee practiced before he formally developed Jeet Kune Do. Some emphasize Original Jeet Kune Do, the art that Lee taught and practiced when he was still alive. Still others offer training in Jeet Kune

Is Certification Necessary?

If instructors are certified, that certainly gives them a measure of credibility and gives you assurance regarding their skill. However, you must also consider the source of the certification. Also, there are many knowledgeable individuals who have the capacity to teach—and may, in fact, be teaching—but are not formally certified. As in many fields, let the buyer beware.

Do Concepts, sometimes teaching other arts separately or blended with some of the Jeet Kune Do techniques. There are those who offer limited training in Lee's original art and emphasize other arts that they like better.

The decision to train with a particular teacher or at a specific school should not be taken lightly, because the teacher or school will greatly influence your understanding of Jeet Kune Do. You should take certain steps in deciding whether or not to train. You should have in mind whether you are interested specifically in studying the actual training methods, techniques, and principles that Lee taught. If so, then you need to make sure that the teacher has sufficient background in the original art and can teach it. You should visit an actual class or training session to see how the teacher relates to students. You should talk to current students to determine what they like and do not like about the training. If one is available, take an introductory class or commit to a trial period to experience the training firsthand. You should also gather information about the instructor's background, experience, lineage, and certification. Most importantly, you should define your training goals and evaluate whether the school or instructor can effectively assist you in meeting those goals.

Group vs. Private Training

A group class provides the opportunity to work out with different types of people with different energy levels, personalities, and so on. Private training involves more personal attention and interaction with an instructor, but usually costs more. It may be a better way to start, however.

chapter 5

the jeet kune
do class

I N ONE SENSE, there is no such thing as a typical Jeet Kune Do class, because students must train in a variety of elements. The art has no set curriculum, no set number of techniques, and no required number of drills. Lee recognized that no two students are alike, so when he taught, every session was different.

Individual instructors, even within the same school, have different teaching styles and approach the material differently. One instructor may emphasize kickboxing, for example, while another may stress trapping. Moreover, the particular interpretation of Jeet Kune Do that an instructor embraces will influence the material taught.

A t the Chinatown Jun Fan Gung Fu Institute, students wore naval-style boxing headgear (with the bar across), boxing gloves or Kempo gloves, kendo armor, and baseball shin guards. While some of the specifics have changed, the basic setup remains the same even today.

An Original Jeet Kune Do Class

That being said, in a class that focuses on Original Jeet Kune Do, there are some common elements that students will often see. Usually students will open the class with the Jeet Kune Do salutation, paying respect to the founder of the art. They may shadow-box and skip rope to help get their blood flowing. Then the instructor, often addressed as *sifu*, will lead the class through stretches and warm-up exercises. Typically, students will do static and dynamic leg stretches to prepare for kicking drills. Also, students will frequently execute stomach exercises, such as crunches.

Some of the equipment that is common in martial arts schools today was pioneered by Bruce Lee. His foam football shield was the forerunner of the kicking shield. The leather focus mitts that he employed foreshadowed the different types of punching mitts available today.

When the warm-up is finished, the instructor will teach students punches and kicks. Students will divide into pairs and practice a specific punch or kick that the instructor shows them. The teacher will carefully monitor the students and correct them individually. Drills can involve single or multiple strikes, depending upon what is being covered. Students use this time to develop their tools and to refine their execution. This part of the class is typically the most challenging from a conditioning standpoint.

The teacher may also teach defensive maneuvers to the students. One student may throw punches or kicks at another student, who practices a specific defensive move against the strike. Counterattack drills may be trained as well, so that students learn to strike or kick in response to being attacked.

Next, the instructor may instruct in close-quarters techniques such as trapping or stand-up grappling. Again, students work in pairs, taking turns practicing the techniques. The instructor will correct students as needed.

At more advanced levels, students may spar. Typically, the instructor will teach drills that emphasize qualities such as timing, rhythm, and distance. Students might be allowed to spar using only certain tools, such as lead hand against lead hand, or lead hand against lead foot. Only when they have sufficient experience will an instructor let students use all of their tools in a freestyle manner.

Gear, Equipment, and Clothing

In Jeet Kune Do students do not practice kata, forms, or strikes in the air. Instead, they strike and kick resistance equipment. To improve speed and accuracy, a student punches and kicks a focus mitt held by a training partner. Focus mitts are superb pieces of equipment that can be utilized in many different ways by an experienced trainer. Students frequently wear bag gloves or open-finger gloves to protect their hands when they strike the focus mitts.

To strengthen power in kicking, trainers hold kicking shields against their bodies so that students can apply their kicks full force without fear of hurting their partner. Some schools also make use of Muay Thai pads, which are heavily reinfoced and can take punishment from hard kicks, elbow strikes, and knee strikes.

For sparring the equipment worn varies according to the intensity of the training. Students must wear a mouthpiece to protect their jaw from the occasional hits to the face. For more intense sparring, protective headgear should

---

Lee believed that learning one or two techniques was enough for a single training session. He thought that once a student began to spar, he would cease trying to accumulate techniques. Instead, the student would devote his time to practicing simple techniques for correct execution.

---

be worn. Students also must wear boxing gloves, with or without hand wraps, both to protect their own hands and to soften any blows that they inflict on their partner. If kicking is allowed during the sparring, then shin guards are recommended. Students may also wear chest armor to protect their upper body from hard punches and kicks. Male students should wear a cup to protect the groin area.

Boxing gloves tend to be unwieldy for trapping training because students need to use their hands and fingers. Open-finger Kempo gloves are better suited for trapping because they allow the fingers to trap and grab. A slight drawback is that they do not have as much padding as boxing gloves for punching. In these situations students should also wear protective headgear, mouthpieces, and perhaps body armor to protect themselves from the punches.

Other types of equipment used for solo training include heavy bags for developing powerful kicks and punches, top and bottom bags that students can use for striking and practicing ducking and slipping, and the *mook jong*, or wooden dummy, employed for trapping and forearm conditioning.

One of the attractive aspects of learning Jeet Kune Do is that no two classes are the same. One week, students might focus on certain kicking drills. Two weeks later, they may be working primarily on trapping. Because a wide variety of skills must be trained, classes tend to cover different material at different times.

Because Jeet Kune Do training is different from classical martial arts training, students do not wear *gi*, uniforms, or colored belts. Instead, students generally wear loose clothing such as T-shirts, tank tops, sweatpants, and shorts. Some schools will require students to wear official school clothing, but the emphasis is still on casual, comfortable clothing. Men are encouraged to wear athletic supporters, while women should wear protective bras.

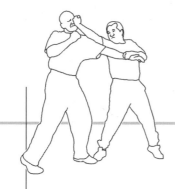

chapter 6
the first
three months

UNFORTUNATELY, many individuals who take up martial arts tend to drop out within the first three months. There are many reasons why a student may quit, including lack of money, change in circumstances, unmet expectations, frustration, boredom, decline in enthusiasm, and distractions. Students initially get excited about becoming good fighters, but when they discover how much work, sweat, and effort is required, they decide the price is too high to pay.

Establishing Good Habits

As with any other athletic endeavor, to become good at Jeet Kune Do, you need to concentrate on learning the fundamentals well. This means working on a proper stance, footwork, and the basic mechanics of your tools. If you learn bad habits in the beginning, you will have to unlearn them later.

Beginning Jeet Kune Do training is no different; in fact, it is probably harder than training in other styles. While other arts may involve having students work on just a few things during the first three months, Jeet Kune Do training requires simultaneous attention to numerous things. For instance, a taekwondo student will typically focus on learning a few kicks during the first three months. In contrast, a Jeet Kune Do student may learn basic punches, kicks, traps, and perhaps grappling during that time. In addition, while other schools primarily stress physical aspects of technique, Jeet Kune Do schools will expect students to understand not only how a technique is executed, but also why and when it is used.

Even though there is no set curriculum in Jeet Kune Do, there is a definite training progression from the basics to more advanced work. As with any other type of athletic endeavor, without strong basics, you will have difficulty

Looking at the Big Picture

Learning Jeet Kune Do, especially in the first few months, is like gathering different pieces of an elaborate puzzle. At first, some of the pieces may seem as if they do not fit together. It is only after working on the art for a period of time that you pick up enough pieces so that an overall picture starts to emerge.

understanding and doing the more sophisticated parts of the art. So it is extremely important for you, as a new student in Jeet Kune Do, to establish a firm foundation in the art that will enable you to make solid progress.

Beginners can expect conditioning to be part of their introduction to Jeet Kune Do. Most classes will introduce students to basic warm-up and stretching exercises to help their muscles become more limber. This not only reduces the risk of injury, but also makes the execution of techniques less difficult. Students will skip rope or shadowbox so that they can increase their endurance.

Formal training will start with learning the *bai-jong*, or ready stance. This is the basis for all the footwork, punching, kicking, striking, trapping, and stand-up grappling that make up the art. It also provides the structure from which you can effectively defend yourself against an opponent's attacks.

From the bai-jong, you will learn fundamental footwork and mobility. You must develop the ability to advance toward an opponent to land a strike and to retreat from an opponent who is attacking. Through footwork training you will begin to understand how to utilize distance against an opponent.

As mentioned, the parts of the body used for striking, primarily the hands and the feet, are known as "tools" in Jeet Kune Do. A very important aspect of initial training is developing these tools so that they can be used with proper form, speed, power, accuracy, and efficiency. Thus, you can expect to devote a great deal of time to focus mitt drills designed to bring forth these skills. You will also practice kicks on kicking shields so that you learn to kick with power. Schools equipped with heavy bags, top and bottom bags, and speed bags will encourage students to train on these, either during class or on their own time.

As a new student you will pay much attention to form and mechanics to instill the proper feeling in your neuromuscular paths. In that way you will learn to move your body correctly, without having to think about it. Understanding the reasons why the body is moved in a certain way, along with repetitive practice, will help instill the movements in your muscle memory, so that they become second nature.

Basic kicks, such as the front snap kick, lead hook kick, and lead side kick, will be introduced as staples of the lower-body tools. Basic punches, such as the lead finger jab, lead jab, lead straight punch, lead hook punch, and rear cross, will also be emphasized. Students will concentrate on executing these techniques as single strikes.

Depending upon the preference of the instructor, you may also start to

Maintaining Enthusiasm

It is natural that a student's initial enthusiasm will wane after a short time. Things that were new soon become routine and familiar. This is the time when you should remember and reaffirm your goals. It is also a time when you need to maintain self-discipline to keep on track towards those goals.

learn simple traps as a beginning student. These may include the *pak sao*, or slapping hand; *lop sao*, or grabbing hand; *jao sao*, or running hand; and *jut sao*, or jerking hand. You will work with a partner and learn how to trap from a reference point, where your arms are already touching.

Finally, you may be introduced to some basic grappling techniques such as neck chokes, locks, or strangleholds.

So, as you can see, within your first few months as a Jeet Kune Do student, you will likely be exposed to many new ideas and techniques that will stimulate your mind and challenge your body.

Many students find training especially challenging in the first few months because they are not used to the physical demands. If you leave your sessions feeling sore and winded, you should not place unreasonable expectations upon yourself. Rather, you need to pace yourself and gradually build up your physical endurance.

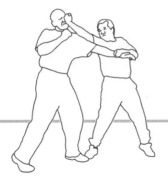

chapter 7
safety

I**T IS VITALLY IMPORTANT** for students learning Jeet Kune Do to train safely in order to minimize the risk of injury. Depending upon the nature and severity of the injury, a student who gets hurt may have to stop training altogether until he or she adequately recovers. Also, a constant threat of injury can discourage students from continuing their training.

Years ago, martial arts instructors did not concern themselves much with safety or student health. It was not uncommon, for example, for students to train barefoot on hard, wooden floors. Students were expected to work out for long periods of time without water breaks. They often sparred hard without much, if any, equipment. They often came away with bruises and cuts, and sometimes with broken bones. Training was what some might consider brutal, and it only appealed to those who were willing to take risks.

Jeet Kune Do instructor Cass Magda recalls that, during the days of the Filipino Kali Academy, students improvised in making their own protective equipment. During the sparring sessions, for instance, instead of wearing a store-bought mouthpiece, students sometimes used mouthpieces made out of toilet paper.

Since then, the martial arts industry has made great strides in terms of safety. Today, the owners and instructors of martial arts schools, including those offering Jeet Kune Do training, are more aware of the need to keep their students healthy and happy. Many schools now have padded floors and mats for their classes. Students are encouraged—indeed, sometimes required—to wear protective gear for more intensive drills or sparring.

More high-quality equipment is available than ever before for Jeet Kune Do

training. Furthermore, improve-
ments in design and manufacturing
have made equipment more dur-
able and easier to use. The hard,
flat, leather focus mitt used in Bruce
Lee's day has given way to scien-
tifically contoured punch mitts with
thick padding. While Lee had to
practice side kicks on a large shield
with a wood backing, nowadays
students utilize heavy foam kicking
shields shaped to readily absorb
kicks. Muay Thai pads have also
made it possible for Jeet Kune Do

> ### How to Avoid Getting Sued
>
> Jeet Kune Do instructors cannot
> afford to ignore safety issues.
> In today's litigious society, stu-
> dents are likely to sue if they are
> hurt because of an instructor's
> negligence. If you become an
> instructor, do not skimp on using
> proper training equipment. Main-
> taining safety may cost money,
> but defending a lawsuit can put
> an instructor out of business.

students to execute their kicks with full power without hurting their partners.

For regular sparring, in addition to boxing gloves, students can wear high-
quality head protectors, padded chest armor, padded groin protectors, and
shin protectors. For full-contact, hard combat, thick padded suits and helmets
are now available that enable the wearers to take strong punishment without
much risk of injury. Indeed, there is almost no excuse for the modern Jeet
Kune Do practitioner not to use at least some safety equipment and gear, given
the wide variety that is readily available.

However, merely having and using high-quality equipment and gear is not
enough. In order to have a safe training experience, you must also follow good
safety habits. For example, two-person drills should be done slowly in the
beginning, to ensure proper form, body feel, and timing and distance. Students should not be allowed to practice the drill at higher speeds until they are
familiar with it and can perform it proficiently.

Training partners should cooperate with each other to ensure that each one
is learning and not getting hurt. If one partner is running through a drill too
quickly, or employing too much power, the other partner should respectfully
ask him or her to slow down to a more comfortable pace. If you believe that
your partner is not paying sufficient attention to your safety, then you should
stop to consult with the instructor or seek a different partner.

Students need to take responsibility for their own safety, as well as that of
other students. Often, you just need to exercise some common sense. For
instance, if you think that a particular drill, technique, or exercise would be

Putting Ego Aside

Injuries can sometimes happen when a student wants to show off. Motivated by pride, such students are more interested in displaying their prowess than in learning and helping their partners to learn. True growth and development, however, can only come when both partners have respect and consideration for each other.

too dangerous for you, you should refrain from doing it. While Jeet Kune Do training is intended to be challenging, you need to be mindful of your own limitations, given your age, level of fitness, flexibility, conditioning, and so forth. You should make sure that you properly warm up and stretch to ensure that your muscles are prepared for training. Cold muscles are more apt to be injured during a workout.

In sparring the risk of injury is higher. You should not engage in sparring until you have developed your tools and can exercise control. Injuries can occur in sparring when students spar too soon, before they have established good control over their bodies. Often students who are inexperienced will let their egos get in the way, and the sparring match becomes a brawl. In such instances students are no longer mindful of each other's safety, but simply want to get the better of their partner.

In summary, safety is everyone's responsibility. Instructors and students must work together to maintain an atmosphere of respect and learning, so that everyone leaves in better condition than when they arrived.

Liability and Assumption of Risk

Although many Jeet Kune Do instructors do not bother with liability forms, a professional school should ensure that all students read and sign them. Such forms should spell out both rights and responsibilities as far as safety is concerned. While the teachers must do all that they can to ensure a safe environment, students themselves must also be vigilant to keep themselves safe, using common sense.

part 3
learning the basics

BEFORE A PERSON CAN RUN, he or she must first learn to stand and to walk. In Jeet Kune Do students cannot effectively execute the more advanced elements, such as the ways of attack, as well as defenses and counterattacks, until they initially learn the basics. Students have to work on the proper way to stand and to move. In addition, they must begin to develop the tools of the trade, namely, the elementary punches, kicks, and other strikes that they will use in fighting.

The fundamentals of Jeet Kune Do will be examined in the next few chapters. We will look at the essential structure of the bai-jong stance, as well as the footwork and mobility that one needs to move in a combat situation. Also, we will closely examine the various upper- and lower-body tools that must be trained so that a student can strike effectively. Finally, some of the basic grappling maneuvers that Bruce Lee researched and incorporated into his fighting method will be discussed.

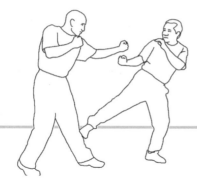

chapter 8
the bai-jong
stance

EACH COMPONENT in Jeet Kune Do is designed to successfully implement the principles of the art. Fundamentally, a proper stance is needed in order to move and to execute the various techniques with speed, power, and precision. Just as other martial arts systems have stances that support the performance of those systems, Jeet Kune Do has a distinctive stance that works with its own method. Bruce Lee carefully thought about the functional capabilities needed when he came up with what is commonly called the *bai-jong*, also known as the "on guard" or "ready" stance (see Figure 8-1).

When Lee first arrived in the United States from Hong Kong, he was still steeped in the Wing Chun system, which has a forward-facing stance that allows for use of both arms. Over the years, as Lee researched and incorporated other techniques and methods, he modified this stance in order to allow for farther-reaching kicks and punches, as well as greater mobility. These capabilities were not needed in the tight quarters of Hong Kong, but they were quite useful in the wider, open spaces of the United States.

Figure 8-1: Bai-jong stance—front view and side view

So the bai-jong grew out of necessity, resulting from Lee's response to changing needs and circumstances. Lee designed the stance to provide for stability and mobility. He wanted to be able to easily evade an opponent's strikes, as well as to advance quickly when attacking. The arts of Western boxing and fencing influenced the bai-jong's hand and foot positions. Lee placed the front and rear hands up as a boxer would, to protect the head and facilitate medium-range punching. He set the feet apart in a way that allows a person to move back and forth and laterally with quickness, like a fencer. Lee placed the stronger side forward, toward the opponent, to pro-

> ### Right vs. Left Lead
>
> Some Jeet Kune Do practitioners prefer a left, or weaker side, lead because Western boxers, Muay Thai fighters, and ordinary street fighters tend to fight from a left lead. However, in his notes, Lee made clear his preference for putting the strong side forward, which, for most, is the right side.

mote striking with the lead hand and kicking with the load foot, much as a fencer places the foil in front. These positions also allow one to protect the centerline and minimize the amount of body exposed to an opponent's attack.

The principle of placing one's stronger side forward dictates that right-handed people will put their right side forward toward an opponent, while left-handed people will do the opposite. Here is an easy way to move into the bai-jong stance from a natural standing position: First, put both feet together, facing forward. Then, assuming that you are right-handed, turn your left foot outward about eighty degrees. Take a forward step with your right foot until your feet are about shoulders' width apart. Those with shorter legs may want to place their feet slightly closer than this, while those with longer legs may want to position their feet a little farther apart than this. Your knees should be slightly bent so that you are in a slightly crouched position, known as the small phasic bent-knee position. This helps your stance to be more stable and grounded when you are momentarily poised between actions. The idea is to achieve a comfortable stance that gives you stability, but also allows you to move freely. The weight should be distributed almost evenly between your feet, so that you feel balanced. As you move, you should maintain a balanced feel so that you are not leaning heavily forward or back, or to the left or right. Although your weight shifts when you execute a particular technique, you

When someone attacks you in the street, there is a good chance you will not be in the bai-jong stance. Instead, you will have to rapidly move into the stance when you have the chance. Therefore, you should practice switching quickly from a natural stance into the bai-jong stance.

will resume a state of equilibrium when you return to the bai-jong.

Your rear foot should not be directly in line behind your front foot. If you draw an imaginary line along the inner side of your front foot, the back of your rear foot should fall just outside that line. The front heel should be turned out slightly, which turns your front knee in so that it protects your groin. Because the front leg is nearer to your opponent, it will do the majority of the kicking and knee strikes. Having the front leg and rear leg positioned in this manner will also facilitate rapid footwork.

Your rear heel should be raised in a cocked position, about 1 to 1½ inches off the ground. This serves several purposes. First, it provides some cushion, allowing you to sink down on your heel and sway your upper body back without moving your feet, if an opponent throws a punch or a high kick at you. Second, with the heel up, you can push off your rear foot for faster footwork and drive. Third, you can move your body weight more powerfully into your punches.

If you are right-handed, your right hand should be in the lead position, facing your opponent. This is because your front hand will do most of the striking and intercepting. Your front arm will be held with the elbow down vertically, about two inches from the ribs. This is known as the immovable elbow position, carried over from Lee's Wing Chun training. When your elbow is down in this way, your forearm will be able to protect your solar plexus and your ribs. The front hand does not remain in a static position, but should move around in small, circular motions between your lead shoulder and your waist. Sometimes the front hand is up, and sometimes it is down. However, it should not be held so high that it obstructs your vision. Also, it should not be held too close to your body, or extended too far away. If it is too close, it will take longer to reach your opponent; if it is extended too far, it cannot generate sufficient power and the arm can tire easily.

Your rear hand is generally held up at chin level and is used mainly for defending against your opponent's attacks. Your rear elbow should be down and pressed close to your body, to protect your left side and kidneys. You do not want to have your rear elbow held out because that would expose your body to your opponent's attack. You use your rear hand to catch or parry strikes that are aimed at your head. If any strikes are thrown at mid-level, you can also drop your rear hand to parry those, or use your rear elbow to cover and protect your midsection. The rear hand can be lowered to protect against low kicks as well.

You can also use your rear hand to throw rear punches, such as a cross or a straight punch. Further, you can use it to trap, or immobilize, your opponent's limbs, or to shoulder-stop your opponent when he or she tries to throw a circular punch. By having your weaker hand in the back, you generate more power when you throw a rear punch, because it has to travel a longer distance to the target. In this way you end up with two strong tools, your forward tool and your back tool, rather than just one strong tool.

 One of the reasons that Lee changed to the more mobile bai-jong stance is that he did not think classical gung fu's "horse stance" and "moving the horse" were helpful. He called them "unnatural rhythmic messes."

With your right hand and right leg nearest to your opponent, the right side of your torso will also face your opponent. You should raise your lead shoulder about an inch or two and tuck in your chin about an inch or two, to help protect your neck from being targeted. Your rear shoulder should be back, but not completely back; if you have it too far back, you cannot use your rear hand for defensive purposes. Having the rear shoulder back presents a smaller target space and also allows longer reach for the front tools to strike their targets. Your upper body should lean forward slightly from the waist to enable you to more easily pull back from an attack. This also gives your opponent's view a false perspective, making your body look closer than it actually is.

While in the bai-jong, you should remain relaxed and calm, avoiding any tension. This will allow you to move and to strike with more power and speed. You will be able to throw punches, kicks, elbow strikes, and knee strikes quickly and efficiently and to return to the ready position rapidly.

The bai-jong can resemble an unorthodox, or left-handed, Western boxing stance, but there are important differences. First, boxers tend to square up

Even when you are momentarily stopped in the bai-jong stance, you should be ready to move instantly. My instructor used to describe this as being like a car that has the engine running, but that is in idle. You need to be already revved up and prepared to take action, without having to first start up.

more, because they use their rear hands more frequently. In contrast, the Jeet Kune Do stance turns the rear side slightly more toward the back, because the emphasis is on using the lead hands. Also, in squaring up, boxers can remain in punching range, and they do not have to worry about being kicked by their opponent. The Jeet Kune Do fighter, on the other hand, is concerned with staying out of range of an opponent's kicks, and must be able to move forward and backwards like a fencer.

Another reason why boxers square up more is that they do no have to worry about being punched or kicked in the groin, because those shots are illegal in the sport. However, in the street the groin is a potential target. Thus, the Jeet Kune Do fighter puts one side forward more and turns the front leg in slightly in order to protect the groin. Boxers can also square up more because they are not allowed to kick. In contrast, the Jeet Kune Do fighters use front kicks as part of their weapons arsenal.

The other major difference is that Western boxers place their weaker side forward and their stronger side in back. Hence, a right-handed boxer will have the left side toward the opponent, while a left-handed boxer will have the right side facing forward. This is because the front hand in boxing is used mostly to probe or to set up for a strong rear-hand punch. In contrast, the Jeet Kune Do fighter places the stronger side forward so that the stronger weapons, which do most of the striking and most of the damage, can reach the opponent more frequently and more quickly.

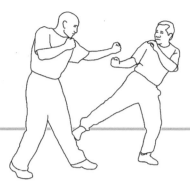

chapter 9
footwork
and mobility

I N A REAL FIGHT, the participants do not simply stand in one place waiting to be hit. They also do not remain in a single position, believing that they will be able to strike their opponent with impunity. In real fighting the participants are moving about, either trying to inflict strikes on each other, or trying to avoid being hit. Moreover, when they do move around, it is usually not from the low, crouching stance that is often associated with traditional martial arts. They are usually standing up, like boxers, running around quickly, chasing each another, or evading each other.

Move Like a Butterfly

B ruce Lee spent hours watching films of the legendary boxer Muhammad Ali, to study his footwork. In *Enter the Dragon*, Lee exhibits the influence of Ali when he dances around his opponent, played by Bob Wall, during their famous fight sequence.

As Bruce Lee matured in his understanding of the true nature of combat, he came to realize the importance of mobility in fighting. So, when he developed the Jeet Kune Do bai-jong, or on-guard stance, he designed it so that the fighter could move quickly in response to the actions of the opponent. He liked the way that fencers were able to advance and retreat rapidly, so he incorporated some of their footwork into his empty-hand method of fighting. Similarly, he appreciated the way that boxers could move around, keeping up on their toes, and staying light on their feet. So Lee also absorbed some of their footwork into Jeet Kune Do.

To be an effective fighter, you must move close enough to the opponent to be able to strike him or her with an appropriate tool, for example, a kick or a punch. Moreover, you must be able to deliver the strike with power, speed, and accuracy, or it will fall short of its intended purpose. Without proper footwork and mobility, you cannot advance toward your opponent in order to accomplish this.

However, being able to advance so that you can attack your opponent is not enough. Your opponent is also going to be attacking you. You need to use footwork and mobility to move away from your opponent so that his or her strikes fall short of landing on you. Not only does this keep you safe, but the failure to connect with you frustrates your opponent psychologically. Emotionally upset opponents are, in some ways, much easier to defend against because they are apt to make more mistakes that you can exploit to your own advantage.

> Lee's private student, Ted Wong, has made it his mission to teach proper Jeet Kune Do footwork. Indeed, he spends more time than any of the other disciples of Lee training students in that aspect of Jeet Kune Do. He considers footwork very important in Jeet Kune Do.

Proper footwork and mobility can also put you into position to counterattack when your opponent tries to strike you. So, rather than going back and forth trading kicks and punches with your opponent, you can strike in the midst of your opponent's attack. This is a more efficient and effective way to deal with an opponent.

In employing any kind of footwork, there are certain qualities that are essential to efficiency and speed. First, you must ensure that you maintain a good sense of balance. You begin with a properly balanced bai-jong stance. As you move into the next position, make sure that you end up in a balanced bai-jong stance. If you lose your balance during your transition, you will not be able to strike from a strong position. Also, from an awkward position, you will not be able to defend well against your opponent's attack. Your opponent can more easily take you to the ground, where you will be more vulnerable.

Second, make sure that your footwork movements are as smooth as possible. That does not necessarily mean that you must move gracefully, because you may occasionally use quick, jerky movements, in what is known as broken rhythm. However, when you move, it should be without clumsiness and without stumbling. You should move without hesitation, unless the hesitation is deliberate. For the most part you should keep your head at an even level as you move, not bobbing up and down, which makes your transition time longer.

Third, when you take steps, make them short and quick. That way, you can move rapidly from one position to the next, ready to go. Avoid lengthy steps that take longer to complete. The longer you are in transition from one spot to the next, the more vulnerable you will be to your opponent's strikes. You are the most stable when both of your feet are on the ground, and the least stable when one or both feet are in transition, not grounded.

Fourth, maintain the integrity of your bai-jong stance when you start and when you end, as well as during your movement, as much as possible. You should keep your hands and arms up as you move, except when you extend your upper body tools to strike. Likewise, you should maintain your small phasic bent-knee position, except when you are using your lower body tools during your movement.

> Lee wanted students to keep moving because they could execute movements more snappily that way than if they started from a position of rest. Opponents, he reasoned, would not be able to guess their intentions because of such movement.

Footwork Movements

From the bai-jong Lee compiled a number of different footwork methods designed to accomplish different purposes. The Jeet Kune Do student should learn the mechanics of each of these types of footwork and practice them often, so that they become as natural as walking or running. The student should also understand the specific circumstances in which each particular type of footwork movement is employed, in order to execute them at the right moment.

Step and Slide Advance

In order to successfully launch an attack upon your opponent, you must be in range to do so. Often, you do not start out in the proper range, so you need to first enter it so that you can attack from there. The step and slide advance is the type of footwork that you would use to close in on an opponent.

From the bai-jong position, you take a step forward with your front foot. Your front heel should land first, followed by the ball of your foot, as in walking. As your weight drops onto the front leg, your rear leg should slide forward, almost gliding along the ground. As it does so, the rear heel should remain in raised position. Your rear leg slides forward until it is the same distance behind your front foot as before. Make sure that, as you complete this series of move-ments, you do not drop and raise your body, but keep your head level. You should be back in the bai-jong, but closer to your opponent.

Because the purpose of this footwork is to enter into the range where you can launch your attack, check your position in relationship to your opponent. If he or she is in your range, then you can attack. If your opponent is still too far away, or has moved away in response to your movement, then repeat the step and slide advance to move into range. It is generally safer to use two or more smaller step and slide movements to close in than it is to use one larger movement, which makes you more vulnerable to counterattack.

> In employing their footwork movements, students must take care to maintain their balance. This is an important part of initial training in order to develop good habits. Although footwork training and maintaining balance may seem tedious, it is necessary to build a strong foundation in Jeet Kune Do.

Step and Slide Retreat

This type of footwork is used to move away from an opponent. You can employ it, for instance, when you want to open the distance between you and your opponent to give yourself more safety. You can also use it when your opponent advances toward you to adjust your distance relative to him or her. If your opponent throws a punch at you, you can take a quick step and slide retreat to avoid the punch. However, you remain in range to easily launch a counterattack, by not moving back too far.

To execute this movement, you begin from bai-jong position and take a small step back with your rear foot. As you land on your rear foot and shift your weight to your rear leg, you slide your front foot back until it is the same distance from your rear leg as before. You should end up in the bai jong, as before, with your weight about evenly distributed between your legs.

Push Shuffle Advance

When you want to launch a medium-range tool, such as a lead finger jab or lead straight punch, you use the push shuffle advance. This type of footwork quickly propels your body weight forward as you execute the technique. The tool then becomes merely an extension of your body, so that you are actually striking with your body, and not merely with your limb.

To execute this footwork, you start from the bai-jong. It is important that your rear heel be raised, because you will launch your forward movement from there (see Figure 9-1). With the heel up, you push off the ball of your rear foot. Your front foot takes a quick forward step as your rear foot moves forward. As you are in transition, your lead tool should already be on the way toward the target. Your tool should hit the target as your front foot is landing, but before it has completely landed. This is known as the principle of "hand before foot." When you hit with your hand before your front foot has stepped down, your body weight is still behind your strike, giving it more power. If your front foot has completely landed before your hand strikes the target, then most of your weight will dissipate down your front leg, making your front hand less powerful.

When you push off your rear foot, make sure that you move your entire body quickly toward your opponent (see Figure 9-2). In that way you improve the chances of your tool striking your opponent. If you move too slowly, your opponent will have more time to see you advancing and can take steps to evade you, or—worse yet—counterattack.

Figure 9-1: From the ready stance

Figure 9-2: Push off the rear foot to move forward

Push Shuffle Retreat

This footwork enables you to quickly move back to avoid your opponent's punch. To execute it from the bai-jong, you raise your front heel slightly so that it is mainly the ball of the foot that is contacting the ground. You then push off the ball of the front foot and propel your body back. As you do so, your rear foot should take a quick step back. The rear foot should land and become settled as your front foot is starting to land.

Slide Step Advance

To launch a kick, such as a side kick, you can employ the slide step advance. This particular type of footwork covers a longer distance than the push shuffle. Therefore, it is better suited for supporting a kick, which is normally executed from a farther distance than a punch. This footwork also covers the distance very quickly, which is necessary in order to successfully land a kick.

To use the footwork to support a kick, you slide your rear foot up until it is behind the heel of your front foot—that is, behind the spot where your front heel was situated before you started to execute the kick. As you slide up your rear foot, your lift your front knee and execute the particular kick that you wish. You should aim to land the kick on the intended target just before your rear foot has settled into its new spot. In this way more of your body weight is behind the kick, which makes it more powerful. Then, immediately after you have kicked your target, drop your front leg so that your front foot is the same distance from your rear foot as before.

Slide Step Retreat

Just as the slide step advance is used to quickly cover much ground, often in conjunction with a lead kick, the slide step retreat is employed to cover a large distance quickly, away from a kicking attack. To defend yourself against a kick, it is better to use this footwork than a push shuffle retreat, because of the longer reach of the opponent's leg. The slide step retreat allows you to move back farther than the push shuffle retreat. Therefore, it increases your chances of evading the kick completely.

To execute this footwork, you slide your front foot back until the heel is right in front of your rear foot. Your rear foot then steps back until the distance between it and the front foot is the same as before. A useful way to develop the timing that is necessary is to have a partner throw kicks at you as you use this footwork to avoid being struck.

Pendulum Step Advance and Retreat

This type of footwork is often confused with the slide step advance and slide step retreat because they are similar, in some ways. Both involve sliding movements of one foot and the displacement of the other. However, while the slide step footwork involves moving your entire body from one spot to the next, the pendulum step involves moving only the feet so that you begin and end in the same spot. There are times when you may wish to kick without shifting to a position closer to your opponent. For example, you may anticipate that, as soon as you execute your kick, your opponent will counter with a kick or a punch. Rather than set down in a closer spot where you can be hit, you may wish to immediately return to your original spot, out of harm's way. In that case, you will want to employ the pendulum step advance and retreat, rather than the step and slide advance.

Starting from the bai-jong stance, you quickly glide your rear foot toward the spot where your front foot sits. As you do so, you quickly raise your front leg and execute the kick, while your rear foot takes the place of your front foot. Your kick should ideally land just before your rear foot settles down, so that more of your body weight is behind the kick. As soon as you strike the target, you quickly retract your front leg. As you do so, your rear foot should glide back to its original spot. Your front foot should then move back into its original spot, so that you end up in the bai-jong, exactly in the place from which you started.

As you execute this footwork, you will notice that your weight quickly shifts to the rear leg as your front leg kicks. Then, as you return, the weight quickly shifts back to the front leg until it is about evenly distributed between the two legs. While your legs are moving from one position to the next, your upper torso should remain in the same place, neither moving forward nor moving back. The end result is that your legs look like a pendulum going back and forth.

Side Step Left

Besides moving forward and backward, you need to develop the ability to move laterally, to the left and to the right. Your opponent may move sideways, so you need to be able to track his or her movement easily. In addition, in certain circumstances, such as having your back against a wall, it helps to know how to move sideways. Stepping sideways also facilitates certain defensive actions, such as slipping a punch, as well as counteroffensive actions, such as throwing a rear cross.

To move sideways to the left from the bai-jong stance, assuming that you lead from the right, your rear foot takes a step to the left. Your lead foot then follows by sliding to the left just enough so that you end up again in the bai-jong (see Figures 9-3 and 9-4). If you want to move a greater distance, it is better to take two small steps in rapid succession than one giant step, which leaves you more vulnerable to your opponent's attack. You should never initiate the movement by stepping with your lead foot, because you will end up momentarily in a cross-step position, which leaves you out of balance.

Figure 9-3: From the ready stance

Figure 9-4: Side step to the left

Side Step Right

To move to the right, your lead foot takes a step to the right. Your rear foot follows by sliding to the right just enough so that you end up again in the bai-jong. To move a greater distance, you should take two small steps in rapid succession rather than one giant step. Do not initiate the movement by stepping with your rear foot, because that will put you in an awkward, unbalanced cross-step position.

Triangle Step Left

There may be times when you want to move diagonally to either side of your opponent. For example, you may want to maneuver to the side as you slip your opponent's punch, then return a hook punch to the kidney area. If you were to use the side step movements, you would most likely be out of range to land your hook punch. So, in this instance a triangle step will move you diagonally to the proper spot. To move to the left, you rotate your right shoulder to the left as your left foot takes a forward step at an approximate forty-five–degree angle. As your left foot completes the step, your right foot can either stay in the same spot or slide slightly forward, depending upon the distance to your opponent. You should end up near your opponent's right side.

Triangle Step Right

A triangle step right is used when you want to move diagonally to the right. To execute this move, you rotate your left shoulder to the right as your right foot steps forward at an approximate forty-five–degree angle. Your left foot will then slide forward slightly so that the distance between your feet remains about the same as before. You should end up near your opponent's left side.

Curving Step Left

This type of footwork is similar to the side step except that you change the angle at which you face an opponent by pivoting. To move to the left, your left foot takes a step to the left. Your right foot follows by sliding to the left. You then pivot on your right foot so that you now face your opponent from an off-angle.

Curving Step Right

To move to the right, your right foot steps to the right. Your left foot then follows by sliding to the right. You then pivot on your right foot and swing your left leg around counterclockwise. You end up facing your opponent from an off-angle.

Step-through Advance

This type of footwork enables you to advance toward your opponent and to change your lead as you do so. Assuming that you begin in a right lead, your left foot steps forward past your right foot. Your left foot should land forward so that you end up in a proper bai-jong stance, but in left lead.

Step-through Retreat

Similar footwork can be employed so that you can retreat from your opponent and end up in the opposite lead. From the bai-jong your lead foot steps back past your rear foot. Your lead foot should land so that you end up in a proper bai-jong stance, but in a different lead.

Steal a Step

This type of footwork is a simple, but deceptive, way to close the distance on your opponent. You subtly bring your rear foot up behind your lead foot, while disguising your action by throwing a fake finger jab or punch to divert your opponent's attention. Because your opponent does not realize that your rear foot is now farther up, he or she does not adjust the distance between you. In effect, you have cut the distance to your opponent by the amount of ground that your rear foot has covered. You can then execute a push shuffle advance to launch a punch or a slide step to launch a kick.

There are other types of footwork that are employed in Jeet Kune Do for different purposes. The footwork discussed here should give the student a solid set of options for moving in relation to the opponent. The student should practice each type of footwork individually. As the student becomes proficient, he or she should then combine the different types of footwork in order to develop the ability to flow from one to the other. A student who can move easily is not only a difficult target to hit, but also a mobile attacker.

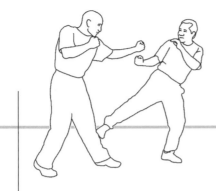

upper-body
tool training

I N ORDER TO BE a successful homebuilder, a carpenter must be familiar with the different implements that are used to construct a house. The carpenter needs to know what each tool does and its purpose. Further, the carpenter has to understand the specific circumstances in which a certain tool should be used.

To be an effective fighter, a Jeet Kune Do student must become familiar with the tools of the trade, namely, the different parts of the body that are used to deliver painful strikes and blows to the opponent's body. The student has to learn the correct mechanics behind each tool and how to properly deliver each tool. Also, the student must refine each tool so that it can be delivered with maximum speed, power, and pinpoint accuracy against a moving target. Without sound training in the use of the tools, the student would be like a carpenter who has a hammer but does not know how to use it to pound a nail.

For ease of organization, the different tools used in Jeet Kune Do can be categorized as either upper-body tools or lower-body tools. The upper-body tools are those that are above the waist, while lower-body tools are those below the waist. The upper-body tools include the hand, elbow, forearm, and head. In the following sections, we will examine these various tools and how to train them.

Hand Tools

Much of the arsenal of the Jeet Kune Do fighter consists of hand strikes. Some of these are delivered using the full extension of the arms, while others are executed when you are closer to the opponent. The entire array of hand strikes covers all the different angles, including overhead, underneath, side, and straight forward. It includes strikes to the head and strikes to the body. A student who trains in the various hand strikes will have a wide range of options for attacking and counterattacking.

Lead Finger Jab

The lead finger jab was reportedly one of Bruce Lee's very favorite tools. It is a deceptively simple technique that can be used by men, women, and children. It does not rely on strength, but rather on speed and accuracy in its delivery.

It might come as a surprise to learn that Bruce Lee held the lead finger jab in very high regard as a weapon. In his notes he wrote, "Faced with the choice of socking your opponent in the head and poking him in the eyes, you go for the eyes every time." (Lee 1997, p. 273)

The lead finger jab perfectly illustrates the principle of aiming the longest weapon at the nearest target. As far as upper-body tools are concerned, the weapons with the longest reach are the fingers, when the lead arm and shoulder are fully extended. The nearest targets are the eyes. The lead finger jab should dart out suddenly, without warning, at the opponent's eyes. The immediate objective is to cause pain and discomfort to the opponent and to disable him or her sufficiently so that you can follow up with other strikes or escape to safety.

To execute the lead finger jab, you start from the bai-jong stance. Your lead elbow should be down, and your lead hand should be facing front. Extend the lead hand forward without turning the elbow out. As you do this, press your fingers together tightly and tuck in your thumb, to form a spear. By collapsing your fingers in this way, you can minimize the chance of hurting your fingers if your strike misses the eyes and hits a harder target instead.

As your arm nearly reaches full extension, rotate your torso at the waist and extend your lead shoulder. This enables your fingers to reach farther so that you can deliver the strike from farther away. After you have extended your fingers as far as they will go, quickly retract the arm with a slight arc to your left. This keeps your arm in constant movement and enables you to bring your arm back to its original position more quickly. You should rapidly resume the bai-jong stance, ready to execute the next strike.

For obvious reasons you cannot practice the finger jab on a live person's eyes.

There are various ways to train at the finger jab without hurting someone. One is to find a training dummy and throw your finger jabs at the head, where the eyes would be. Another is to have a partner hold up a focus mitt with two "eyes" taped on to represent your targets. A third way is to have your opponent wear protective goggles, which you can target with your finger jab.

> **Crispy and Uncrispy Punches**
>
> Jeet Kune Do instructor Tim Tackett likes to describe punches as being either "crispy" or "uncrispy." Crispy, also known as snappy, punches are lighter punches that emphasize speed and rapid hitting. Uncrispy, or heavy, punches are slower, but they load up on power. Both are important ways to execute your punches.

There is a useful drill for training your speed and nontelegraphic movement. As you face your partner, throw out your lead arm as if to do a finger jab. However, instead of striking your partner's eyes, extend your fingers and slightly tap the top of your partner's forehead. Your partner's task is to recognize when you are about to strike and to parry your strike or take evasive action to prevent you from tapping his or her forehead. Your can start the drill from close range, where you do not need to use footwork to move in. Later, you can start from farther back, which forces you to use a push shuffle to advance toward your opponent.

Lead Jab

The lead jab is similar to the Western boxing jab. It is used to gauge one's distance from the opponent. The lead jab is also employed as a probe, to test the opponent's reactions and how he or she moves. In addition, it is also utilized to set up the opponent for follow-up strikes.

To execute the lead jab from the bai-jong stance, you extend your hand out toward your opponent. You turn your arm so that your hand lands in a horizontal fist position, striking the target with the first two knuckles. The punch should be delivered with a snap at the end. Because of the way your arm torques, your lead elbow turns outward. As soon as you strike the target, you retract the arm along the same path, back into the ready position.

Lead Straight Punch

This is considered the basic backbone punch of Jeet Kune Do. Like the lead jab, it can be used to probe, gauge distance, and set up for other strikes. However, by design, it is intended to be a knockout punch. When Bruce Lee developed this punch, he wanted to make it as powerful as, if not more powerful than, the rear punch favored by most fighters as the knockout punch.

In many fighting systems the rear punch is usually more powerful than the lead punch because the rear punch must travel a longer distance to reach the target. In order to make the lead straight punch just as, if not more, powerful, the Jeet Kune Do practitioner must develop the correct body mechanics.

From the bai-jong stance you shoot your front hand forward at a slightly upward angle toward your opponent's face. It is important to keep your elbow down as you do so, not turned out. As you reach for your target, rotate your hips, turn your waist, pivot on your front foot, and extend your lead shoulder. When the punch is executed with proper form, your fist, arm, and both shoulders should be aligned (see Figure 10-1).

Your fist snaps up slightly at the wrist just before striking the target. Your last three knuckles should be the ones that hit the target, in a whip-like fashion. Immediately afterwards, you should continue the motion by curving your fist a few inches to the left and retracting your arm back into ready position. This slight curving to the left is known as the short arc principle. It facilitates the snapping and whipping of the punch and allows you to quickly bring back

Figure 10-1: Lead straight punch on focus mitt

your arm into ready position. If you eliminated the short arc movement at the end of the strike, your arm would have to stop and reverse course in order to get back to ready position. The short arc principle allows you to keep your arm in motion so that you can bring it back more quickly.

Lead Hook Punch

Another technique borrowed from Western boxing, the lead hook punch is designed to strike the side of your opponent's body or head. Common target areas include the ribs, jaw, and temple. It is usually thrown from a slightly closer distance to your opponent and often follows a jab, straight punch, or rear punch as a finishing blow. It can also be thrown as a counter against an opponent's attack.

To execute the punch, raise your lead arm and raise the elbow outward. Your lead fist should move to the side of your opponent's body or head, depending on your target. Swing the punch so that your fist hits the target, making sure that your elbow is up so that your arm is parallel to the ground. Your fist and wrist should be aligned with your lower arm. At a farther distance a vertical fist position works better. However, at a closer distance, either a vertical fist or a horizontal fist position can succeed. Your rear hand should be up with your arm pressed against your side, to protect your head and body.

To generate maximum power behind the punch, you should rotate your hips. Also, your rear heel should slam down as you raise your front heel and pivot on the ball of your foot. Imagine that the front of your lead foot is nailed to the ground, so that, when you pivot, your lead heel cannot help but go up.

One error to avoid is swinging the punch at an upward diagonal angle, rather than along a straight, horizontal plane. That will only serve to weaken the punch because the arm is not properly aligned along the path of the punch. Another error to avoid is overextending your punch past the centerline. By doing so, you expose your body to a counterattack. Instead, make sure that, as soon as you hit your target, you quickly retract your lead arm back into ready position.

Lead Backfist

Just as the hook punch strikes one side of head, the lead backfist hits the other side of the head. This particular punch utilizes the hinging motion of your lead elbow to whip your lead arm so that your fist strikes your opponent's face. The knuckles of your fist should strike soft-tissue areas such as the nose, jaw, and ear. Avoid landing on the temple or other hard parts of the skull, which can break your knuckles.

The lead backfist can be thrown from normal punching range. However, it is often executed as part of a hand immobilization attack or progressive indirect attack.

Refining the Tools

Ted Wong, one of Lee's private students, has said that it took him about six months to learn the lead straight punch. But it took him another twenty years to perfect it. While the basic mechanics of any punch can be learned in a short time, you have to spend hours practicing it in different contexts to make it useful and effective.

Lead Uppercut

Another technique incorporated from Western boxing, this particular punch is thrown when you are close to your opponent. The mechanics are similar to those of the lead hook punch. However, instead of executing the punch horizontally, you throw it at an upward angle to strike the bottom of your opponent's chin or solar plexus. You must make sure that your fist, wrist, and arm are aligned in a straight line when you throw the punch. Your knuckles should face your opponent.

You should start with your front hand tucked in close to your chin. Just before you start to launch the punch, bend your knees and drop slightly, keeping both hands close to your chin. As you throw the punch, push off from the heel of your front foot and straighten your front leg, which raises your hip. Your rear heel should drop down. The punch should go up in a straight line through the target area.

Avoid a wide, looping movement when you throw the punch. That type of movement uses mostly arm power, rather than the power of your entire body. It also takes longer for the punch to reach the target and telegraphs the punch as well.

Lead Shovel Hook

The shovel hook is similar to the lead hook punch, but it is thrown from about hip level and strikes the lower part of the body. Typical target areas for the shovel hook are the stomach, lower ribs, side, and kidney area. The execution of the punch resembles the action of shoveling dirt or snow.

The power comes from rotating your front hip as you lift your front heel and push up from the ball of your front foot. As you launch the punch, be sure to keep your rear arm against your body with your hand protecting your chin.

Rear Cross

As important as the lead hand is for most of your attacks, the rear hand also comes into play at appropriate times, especially for a finishing, or knockout, blow. One of the most important rear-hand techniques is the rear cross, borrowed from Western boxing.

With your rear hand starting near your chin, you extend the rear arm and turn the rear hand into a horizontal fist. At the same time you bring your lead arm back and press it against your body, keeping your lead hand up to protect your face. You push off your rear foot and torque your hips as you continue to throw the rear fist toward the target.

The rear cross can strike either the head or the midsection of your opponent. You bend your front leg and bring up the rear leg slightly while executing the punch. Also, extend the rear shoulder to maximize the reach of your arm for penetrating power. In addition, you dip your torso slightly into the punch and lower your chin to help protect your head against any counterpunch.

> ## One Tool, Many Uses
>
> **E**very upper-body tool that you train can be applied in different ways and situations. For instance, the lead straight punch can be used offensively in each of the five ways of attack. It can be used as a counterattack, for example, to intercept an opponent. You can fire it as you move forward, backward, left, or right.

Because the punch begins from the rear, it travels a longer distance to the target. During that time, it is able to generate more power, so that the resulting strike can be devastating. In his notes Bruce Lee compared the execution of the rear cross to slamming a door.

The rear cross is usually thrown in combination with a lead punch, such as the lead jab or lead straight punch. When it connects, the lead punch momentarily stuns the opponent, opening the way for the rear cross to be fired to knock out the opponent. This effective combination is often referred to as the "one-two."

Rear Overhand

The rear overhand is similar to the rear cross, but your rear arm follows an upward arc instead of a straight path to the target. The punch is thrown when you are facing a taller opponent, because the upward arc enables your punch to reach your opponent's head. Also, it is useful for countering an opponent's lead punch, because it can arch over and above the punching arm to strike the opponent in the head.

Rear Straight Punch

The rear straight punch is fired straight out. Instead of turning the rear hand into a horizontal fist, you turn it into a vertical fist. You torque your hips and extend your rear shoulder as you punch. However, it does not penetrate as deeply as the rear cross, so it is more appropriate when you are closer to the opponent.

This type of punch is typically thrown in two situations. When your opponent throws a lead straight punch at you from matched lead (for example, if you are in right lead and your opponent faces you in right lead), your rear arm can punch across your opponent's arm, which is known as a sliding leverage punch. Also, when you grab and pull your opponent's lead arm, as in trapping, you can throw the rear straight punch at his or her head.

Rear Uppercut

The rear uppercut is similar to the lead uppercut, except that it uses the rear arm and hand. It is thrown when you are closer to your opponent. With the rear hand positioned by your chin, you dip your body and bend your knees slightly (see Figure 10-2). You then throw the punch at an upward angle, targeting either the bottom of your opponent's chin or the solar plexus.

Figure 10-2: Rear uppercut to focus mitt

The power comes from pushing off the ball of your rear foot and turning up your rear hip as you throw the punch. Like the lead uppercut, the rear uppercut should not be a wide, looping punch, which would take longer to reach the target and telegraph your intentions.

Figure 10-3: Lead forearm strike

Figure 10-4: Rear elbow strike against Thai pad

Forearm Strikes

As we move down along the arm, we find that another useful striking tool in some circumstances is the forearm. You can strike with either the inner forearm or the outer forearm. Also, you can employ a lead forearm strike or a rear forearm strike. It can follow another strike, such as a punch. Some potential targets include the face, neck, or chest (see Figure 10-3).

Elbow Strikes

At close range elbow strikes are very effective techniques against your opponent. You can throw either a lead or a rear elbow. The strikes can also come from different angles. For instance, you can execute the elbows upward, which will generally target your opponent's chin or solar plexus. Another option is throwing them forward horizontally, striking the temple or chin of your opponent. You can also hurl them diagonally up or down against your opponent's face (see Figure 10-4). Further, you can throw them horizontally or diagonally to strike someone behind you. Finally, you can slam them downward, for example, into the back of your opponent's neck if he is bent down.

Headbutt

A rarely used, but quite damaging tool is the headbutt. This is applied at close range when you can slam the scalp portion of your head against your opponent's face. The collision between your hard skull and the soft tissue of your opponent's face can inflict serious injury on your opponent. For that reason it should be used only in the gravest of circumstances when such force is reasonable and justified.

These represent some of the important, basic upper-body tools that you should develop in order to maximize your ability to deliver strikes from various angles and distances. In the early stages you should concentrate on good form, solid body mechanics, strong power, and rapid speed. Working these tools is part of establishing a firm foundation in Jeet Kune Do.

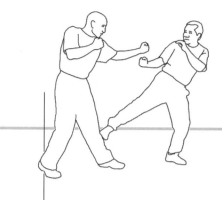

lower-body tool training

MANY MARTIAL ARTISTS, including Jeet Kune Do practitioners, feel most comfortable employing upper-body tools, particularly the hands, as the primary weapons. This is natural and to be expected, because we use our hands for most of our daily tasks. We generally employ our legs and our feet for standing or walking.

However, if we focus only on the upper-body tools, we miss out on some important weapons that can prove very useful in combat. The lower-body tools provide additional options that the Jeet Kune Do fighter can employ to become a well-rounded fighter. Many street fighters themselves are not well trained in deploying, or defending against, the lower-body tools. The Jeet Kune Do fighter who can make intelligent use of these weapons can gain an advantage over an opponent.

> Lee acknowledged that, under normal circumstances, training the legs was more difficult than training the hands. He reasoned that people use their hands more often than their legs. Also, less energy is consumed in using the hands to strike, because the power of the waist can be employed.

The lower-body tools consist of long kicks, short kicks, and knee strikes. Like the upper-body tools, these lower-body techniques can be delivered from different angles, such as left side, right side, and straight. They can be executed from different heights, namely, high, middle, and low, although the main emphasis in Jeet Kune Do is on striking low.

Kicks

Because most people have two feet, it makes sense that Bruce Lee would want to incorporate kicks that employ both feet. He researched different kicks from

Northern gung fu styles and French Savate to develop his arsenal of kicks. As a result, Jeet Kune Do contains both lead kicking tools and rear kicking tools. However, the stress is on the lead tools about 80 percent of the time in attacking, so the lead kicks are utilized much more often than the rear kicks. The following is an examination of some of the major kicks included in Jeet Kune Do.

Lead Snap Kick

In a street confrontation the basic rule is that there are no rules. For good reasons sporting matches prohibit strikes to the eyes, knees, and groin, but these targets are considered fair game in a real fight. In particular, kicks to the groin are part of the arsenal of the Jeet Kune Do fighter.

The lead snap kick is one of the basic kicks that aim for your opponent's groin. To deliver this kick, you raise your front knee and lift your front foot off the ground. From there you snap the lower leg in an upward, vertical line so that your front foot strikes your opponent's groin. Your instep or tip of the foot should make contact with the groin. It should strike the target like a whip.

In his films Bruce Lee became famous for his rapid, high kicks to the head. However, for a real street fight, he would discourage the use of such kicks, instead opting for targets at the middle to lower levels of the body. This is because a person can easily lose his balance if he tries a high kick on the street.

If you are already in range to strike your opponent's groin, then you only need to shift your weight back to your rear leg as you lift your front leg to execute the kick. However, if you are initially out of range of your target, then you can use slide step footwork to put you into position to land the kick. After doing so, you can drop your front foot to the ground so that you are close enough to follow up with a lead punch. Alternately, if you do not want to stay at that distance—for example, because you want to avoid a counterattack—then you should use pendulum footwork. This will enable you to land the snap kick, then quickly return to your original position.

Lead Inverted Kick

This particular kick is similar to the lead snap kick in its mechanics. However, it is used specifically against an opponent who is in an unmatched lead. For example, if you are in right lead and your opponent faces you in left lead, you can utilize this kick.

When your opponent is in unmatched lead, the primary targets for your strikes, such as the sternum and groin, face away from you. Therefore, your strikes must come from a different angle in order to reach them. While many kicks tend to move from the outside in, the lead inverted kick moves from the inside out, in order to reach these targets. It can be compared to the lead back-fist, which also moves from the inside out.

To execute the lead inverted kick, lift your knee as you would for the lead snap kick. Then tilt your knee outward toward your right. From there snap the lower leg so that it goes along an outward angle and your front foot can strike your intended target (see Figure 11-1). As soon as your foot has landed on the target, retract it along the same line and drop your foot down so that you are closer to your opponent. If you do not want to land in a closer posi-

Figure 11-1: Lead inverted kick against focus mitt

tion, you can bring your foot back to its original position.

The lead inverted kick can be thrown from a stationary position if you are in range to reach your target. Otherwise, you can use slide step advance footwork to bring you into range. You can also employ pendulum step footwork to reach the target, then return to your initial position.

Lead Hook Kick

The lead hook kick is another technique in which you snap the lower leg into the target. Like the hook punch, it travels along a horizontal angle from the

> **"So** many people concentrate on their hands and neglect the training of their legs. If our footwork and kicks are good, the area of attack will be widened. The attacking power of the legs is greater than fists. You will know it simply when you look at them—the legs are bigger than the arms." (Lee 1997, p. 323)

side into your opponent's body. In some ways it is similar to the roundhouse kick used in other martial arts systems. However, the lead hook kick does not chamber, or cock back, as much before it snaps at the target. Also, it moves along a tighter arc toward the target and is more explosive. It should not swing along a wide arc because that exposes your body too much to counterattack.

To execute this kick, you first lift your lead knee. You then turn your body toward the side and torque your hips as you aim the lead knee toward the target. You should pivot on your rear foot as you snap your lower leg. The top instep of your front foot should make impact with your target. As soon as it does, you retract your lower leg along the same line and drop your knee. Your front foot then drops down, and you should return to the bai-jong stance.

The lead hook kick can be executed at different heights, depending upon your intended target. A high hook kick can strike the head. A mid-level hook kick can hit the ribs. A low hook kick can target the groin, inner thigh, or knee. Depending upon your flexibility, you should practice the hook kick at varying levels, which gives you more options and makes it more difficult to predict where you will kick.

You can throw the lead hook kick from a stationary position if you are already in range to land the kick upon your opponent. Otherwise, you utilize slide step footwork to move into range to land the kick. Alternately, you can use pendulum footwork to land the kick and then return to your original position, safe from your opponent's counterattack.

Lead Side Kick

The lead side kick has the longest reach of any kick and was one of Bruce Lee's specialties. He refined it to the point where it was the most powerful kicking tool in his arsenal. Although many believe that the side kick is a relatively slow and telegraphic kick, Lee could execute it with such speed and power, even from a stationary position, that his opponents could not avoid being struck.

In throwing the lead side kick, especially from long range, you must commit the entire weight of your body into the forward motion. When this is done properly, the momentum generated by the kick can send your opponent flying back, with little chance of recovery. However, you must execute it with the right timing, lest your opponent evade the kick and counterattack in the midst of your completing it.

To execute the kick, you raise your front knee. You must turn your body to the side and torque your hips so that your entire body is aligned toward the target. Your rear foot should pivot. You then thrust the leg from your hips into the target. Your lead foot should turn so that it is parallel to the ground from toe to heel. The surface of the foot that strikes the target should be the bottom flat portion of the foot, not the edge.

As you extend your leg into the target, your upper torso should lean back to assist in the proper alignment of the entire body (see Figure 11-2). This also moves your upper body away from any counterattacks that your opponent may attempt. Further, it provides a counterbalance to your extended kick.

The kick can be thrown at either mid-level or low level. At mid-level your target is your opponent's chest or stomach. At low level, the knee or shin is a useful target.

You can throw the kick from a stationary position if you are already in range. If your opponent advances toward you, you can use the side kick to counter his or her forward movement. If your opponent is in long range, use slide step footwork to advance toward your opponent as you execute the kick.

Figure 11-2: Lead side kick against kicking shield

Lead Thrust Kick

The lead thrust kick propels your foot along a forward horizontal line to your opponent, which pushes him or her backward. To execute the kick, you raise your front knee and front hip to cock the leg. Normally, your rear shoulder will move forward so that you face your opponent in a more squared-up position. From there, with your lower leg hoisted and front toes pointed up, you use your hip to thrust the front foot forward. The ball of your foot strikes your opponent to knock him or her back.

This particular kick can be thrown at mid-level or low level. At mid-level you target either the sternum or the midsection. At low level you aim for the thigh or the knee. Rather than retract the lead leg, you usually drop the leg down after completing the kick. This takes you closer to your opponent, so you can follow up with other techniques as needed. While executing the kick, be sure to keep both of your hands up, both to protect yourself and to keep them in position to strike.

Lead Foot Obstruction

This particular kick illustrates the principle of interception in Jeet Kune Do. It looks similar to a side kick to the shin, but it is executed differently. As an opponent in long range steps toward you to punch or kick, you turn your hips and lift up your front leg so that your front foot is turned sideways. Keep your leg stiff as the front foot targets your opponent's front shin. In this manner you obstruct the forward movement of your opponent, disrupting the attack, which allows you to follow up with a lead hand attack. You can also use this kick in a preemptive manner as you advance toward your opponent, to prevent him or her from using the lead leg to counterattack you as you move forward.

Rear Hook Kick

Besides the lead hook kick, there is also a rear hook kick, which moves from the outside in to the target. The mechanics are similar to those of the lead hook kick, except, of course, that the kick emanates from the rear leg instead of the front leg. To execute it, you lift your rear knee and turn your body to the side. You torque your hips and snap the lower part of the leg so that the instep of your rear foot strikes the target (see Figure 11-3). As you turn into the kick, you pivot on your front foot.

Figure 11-3: Rear hook kick against Thai pad

To complete the kick, you can set your rear foot down so that you end up in a different lead. You can also retract your foot so that you end up in your original position. However, doing so can be relatively slow because of the longer distance that the foot must cover in returning.

Rear Thrust Kick

Like the lead thrust kick, this particular kick begins with raising the rear hip and rear knee forward. From there you lift up the lower part of your rear leg so that your rear toes point up. You use your rear hip to thrust your leg forward to strike at your opponent. The ball of the foot strikes your opponent, sending him or her backward. Although it is possible to retract the leg after the kick, the momentum of the kick normally brings your rear leg forward in front of your other leg. It is easier, therefore, to simply drop the foot and end up with the other side forward.

Because the distance of your kick is dictated by the position of your front support leg, the rear thrust kick has a greater reach than the lead thrust kick. If your opponent is too far away for you to strike with a lead thrust kick, you may be able to reach your target with the rear thrust kick.

Spinning Rear Kick

Another kick that makes use of the longer reach of the rear leg is the spinning rear kick. To execute this kick, you first turn your body away from your opponent as you pivot on your front leg. As you continue to rotate your body, turn your head forward so that you are looking at your opponent over what was previously your rear shoulder.

You want to be able to see where your opponent is. While continuing to

The kicking in Jeet Kune Do is not supposed to be like slugging it out with the fists. My teacher related something that his own instructor used to say—namely, that we should learn to box with our feet. Rather than swinging like a baseball bat, a kick should hit with precision, like a hammer.

pivot, you raise your rear knee and leg in a cocked position. Then you thrust the foot forward, toes pointing sideways as in a side kick.

This kick can be used in several different ways. It can be employed as a surprise attack on an opponent who believes he or she is safe, just outside of range of your lead leg. While your opponent expects you to throw a lead kick, you can suddenly pivot on your front foot, spin, and thrust the rear foot to strike your target.

Another use is as a follow-up to a lead leg attack. For example, suppose you throw a lead hook kick at your opponent that barely misses, because your opponent retreats. Rather than do another lead leg attack, which the opponent may also evade, you can execute the spinning rear kick to reach your opponent.

A third use of this kick is as a counterattack to an opponent's lateral movement. Suppose you face your opponent with your right side forward, when he or she suddenly darts diagonally to the left. Rather than change your position to try to track this movement, you can pivot on your lead foot and throw the spinning rear kick while your opponent is in transition.

Rear Oblique Kick

The rear oblique kick strikes the opponent's front knee or shin with the arch of your rear foot. You can use it as either an attacking motion or an intercepting motion. For attacking, you lift your rear knee and turn your foot so that your toes face outward. Then thrust the kick at a slightly downward angle into your opponent's front knee or shin.

To intercept, rather than lift up the rear knee, you glide it in an upward arc so that the foot lands on the target to stop your opponent's forward movement. In either case, after landing the kick, you retract the leg to its original spot so that you remain in the same position as before. If your opponent steps back after you land the kick, however, you can set down your rear foot and shift your weight onto it as you step forward with the other foot, so that you move up toward your opponent. Alternately, you can kick with your lead foot after setting down your rear foot.

Knee Strikes

The knee is a lower-body tool that is typically used at close range. Both the front knee and the rear knee can be used to strike an opponent. Knee strikes can be executed along different angles. Either knee can be driven upward

Figure 11-4: Lead knee strike against Thai pads

into the opponent—for example, as you pull your opponent's torso down toward you. If you pull your opponent's upper body to the side, you can drive your knee in an inward fashion into the body.

The knee can also shoot forward to strike your opponent's legs. Finally, if your opponent is on the ground, you can drive the knee downward into the opponent.

The lower-body tools provide additional striking options that you can implement, particularly when you are at a farther distance from your opponent. In addition, they can be used to set an opponent up for different hand techniques. They enable the Jeet Kune Do student to become well-rounded and versatile.

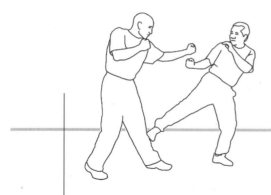

chapter 12
grappling

I N THE LATTER PART of the twentieth century, many students, particularly in the United States, were captivated by the grappling craze. Schools offering training in arts such as Brazilian jujitsu, shoot wrestling, Russian *Sambo*, and Greco-Roman wrestling sprang up. Martial artists from many systems started to recognize that they needed to learn how to grapple in order to be well-rounded and competitive.

Perhaps the best-known grappler with whom Bruce Lee trained was "Judo" Gene LeBell. The latter's wrestling knowledge and experience influenced Lee's own development in the grappling area. Even today, LeBell continues to inspire martial artists throughout the world.

Although the need to know grappling did not become apparent to many students until recently, Bruce Lee had already realized this back in the 1960s. As he endeavored to become a versatile fighter, he researched and studied numerous grappling systems. These included aikido, wrestling, judo, and jujitsu. He worked out with some talented grapplers of the day, tapping into their understanding and experience.

However, unlike some of the arts widely practiced today, which focus almost exclusively on grappling and ground fighting principles and techniques, Lee's system never over-emphasized grappling to the virtual exclusion of any other fighting method. Lee regarded clinging to a particular style of fighting as "partiality," or having only a segment of the truth. Instead, Lee strove for "totality" in combat, an ability to fight in all ranges and to utilize all tools and methods. Grappling was just one facet of fighting that Lee sought to understand.

In contrast to the kicking, punching, and trapping aspects of Jeet Kune Do, the grappling aspects were never developed into a comprehensive methodology. Indeed, even as he studied grappling during the latter period of his life, Lee rarely, if ever, taught it at the Los Angeles Chinatown Jun Fan Gung Fu Institute or to most of his private students. However, he had a large collection of books on aikido, judo, jujitsu, and wrestling, and he made notations and drawings in many of them. He documented much of his research in his personal notes. Lee also experimented with grappling methods with Dan Inosanto, his private student and assistant instructor at the Chinatown school. In addition, one of his students from the school, Larry Hartsell, went on to do considerable research into grappling methods. Much of the material that is regarded as Jeet Kune Do grappling has been passed on through these various sources. The result is a comprehensive collection of different grappling skills that fits in with the rest of the art of Jeet Kune Do.

The Philosophy of Jeet Kune Do Grappling

A useful way to understand the philosophical approach to grappling in Jeet Kune Do is to compare and contrast it with the general approach of various systems widely practiced today. Most students of modern grappling arts study ways to fight with an opponent while both are on the ground. Indeed, these systems encourage students to take their opponents to the ground and to use their skills to keep their opponents subdued until they submit.

The objective of the Jeet Kune Do fighter is to avoid going to the ground with an opponent. Rather, the Jeet Kune Do practitioner generally aims to take an opponent to the ground without accompanying him or her there. Once the opponent is on the ground, the Jeet Kune Do fighter will either escape or assume a superior position to keep the opponent at a disadvantage. A Jeet Kune Do fighter will not seek to wrestle with an opponent who is on the ground.

Also, many systems today are practiced with an orientation toward sport and competition. They stress submission holds and locks that are designed to apply pressure

Defending against Grappling

Lee did not study grappling just to learn how to use it against an opponent. He also studied it so that he could figure out ways to defend against it. Since there are so many skilled grapplers these days, a Jeet Kune Do student needs to learn how use his various skills to deal with them without being taken to the ground.

The influence of grappling on Bruce Lee can be seen in his films. In the opening fight sequence of *Enter the Dragon*, Lee finishes off his opponent with an arm lock. Lee also defeats Kareem Abdul-Jabbar in *Game of Death* by strangling him. In *The Chinese Connection*, Lee defends against an opponent's scissor-legs choke by biting his leg.

until the opponent gives up. The grappling in Jeet Kune Do emphasizes effectiveness in street altercations. The techniques are intended for real self-defense applications, where one's life and safety depend upon their effectiveness. Rather than methodically flowing from one position and technique to another until an opponent submits, the Jeet Kune Do fighter seeks to use grappling to quickly end the fight.

Grappling techniques in Jeet Kune Do fall into several categories. These include single-leg attacks, double-leg attacks, throwing, and tackling. Leg locks, arm locks, and neck locks are also part of these techniques. In addition, chokes, strangleholds, controls, and manipulations are part of the grappling arsenal. Some of these techniques are discussed below.

Leg Attacks

Double-Leg Takedown

To execute this type of takedown, you must drop down, grab both of your opponent's legs, and hoist them off the ground so that your opponent falls backwards. As you lift your opponent's legs, you also drive your shoulder forward into your opponent. This facilitates the takedown and prevents opponents from moving back and shifting their weight to keep their feet on the ground.

The double-leg takedown is best executed against an opponent whose legs are more squared up toward you. This makes it easier for you to wrap your arms around your opponent's legs.

There are various ways to enter into a double-leg takedown. For example, you can use your hands to bump up your opponent's arms to clear the way for you to grab his or her legs. If you do a double jut sao, or downward jerking motion of your opponent's arms, your opponent may react by resisting and moving his or her arms up—which can also open up the way for you to grab your opponent's legs. You can feint a hand attack toward your opponent's face—for example, a lead finger jab—to draw your opponent's arms upward for protection against your strike. This too will allow you to drop into a double-leg takedown. You can fire a combination of punches to the head, causing your opponent to raise his or her arms for protection, and you can then shift downward into the double-leg takedown. There are many ways to move into a position from which you can execute the takedown successfully.

In addition, there are several follow-up lock positions that you can use after taking your opponent down onto his or her back. You continue to hold on to both legs, placing your opponent's feet behind your armpits, and wrap your forearms tightly around your opponent's ankles, Achilles tendons, or knees. You then pull upward and squeeze to lock your opponent's legs.

From there you yourself can sit on the ground. You lean back and continue to pull on the legs while squeezing. Alternately, instead of sitting down, you can turn your opponent over, face down, which means that you are now facing away from him or her. You then sit down near your opponent's rump as you bend his or her legs and squeeze.

Single-Leg Takedown

This type of takedown works best against a person who has one leg predominantly in forward position. You execute this takedown by dropping down and

Figure 12-1: Single-leg takedown

grabbing hold of your opponent's front lower leg, close to, or at, the ankle. Your rear hand pulls up on the lower leg to bring your opponent off-balance. You can use your lead hand to grab your opponent's thigh to assist in pulling up the leg. Alternately, you can brace your front outer forearm against your opponent's front knee as you pull up on his or her lower leg (see Figure 12-1).

As you pull up on your opponent's leg, you step up and set your front foot in back of your opponent's support leg. From there you drive your shoulder forward into your opponent so that he or she trips on your front leg and falls backwards onto the ground.

From this position you can apply a lock against the knee, Achilles tendon, or ankle. While continuing to hold your opponent's lead leg, you brace the bottom of your closest foot against the thigh of your opponent's free leg. This prevents him or her from using the free leg to kick or bother you. Wrap your rear arm around the ankle of the front leg and brace your lead hand against the leg. Then straighten yourself and pull up on the leg as you squeeze to lock it into place. From there you can sit down while maintaining your lock on your opponent's leg and pressing your foot against the thigh to keep him from kicking you.

There are different ways to enter into the single-leg takedown. For example, suppose you fire a lead jao sao, or running hand, toward your opponent's temple. If your opponent does an outward block with the rear arm, you can quickly drop down and strike your opponent's groin with your lead hand. You wrap your left hand behind your opponent's front ankle and press your right forearm against his or her front knee. Then pull up on the leg and drive your opponent forward so that he or she falls backward.

As another illustration, suppose that your opponent faces you in unmatched lead. He or she throws a front-hand hook punch, which you evade by ducking under it. As you duck, your rear hand grabs the back of your opponent's front ankle, while your front hand grabs the upper thigh. You then pull up the leg and drive your shoulder forward into your opponent, sending him or her backwards onto the ground.

As in the case of the double-leg takedown, you can feint a lead finger jab to draw your opponent's arms upward. With the lower area cleared, you can drop down and grab your opponent's front leg, using both of your hands. You lift up the leg and drive your opponent off-balance so that he or she falls to the ground.

Throws

Bruce Lee incorporated a number of throwing techniques from the Japanese martial arts into his Jeet Kune Do. One of them, *osoto gari*, involves tripping your opponent onto the ground. For example, from a lead hand attack, your lead hand lop saos, or grabs, your opponent's front arm and pulls. As you pull, you fire a rear straight punch to the face to stun your opponent. You then step in with your front leg behind your opponent's front leg. Your lead arm does a forearm smash against the upper body, and your front leg kicks back to trip up your opponent's front leg (see Figure 12-2). You propel your upper body forward and downward against your opponent's upper body, to force him or her backward onto the ground.

Figure 12-2: Osoto-gari throw

Another technique, *tai otoshi*, is essentially a hip throw. As your rear hand pulls your opponent's lead hand forward, your lead hand twists your opponent's neck. You turn and pivot on your rear leg, placing your front leg behind your opponent's front leg. You then continue to pull the arm and twist the neck, while striking your front leg into the back of your opponent's front leg to throw him or her over your hip and onto the ground.

Arm Locks

Another category of grappling skills involves arm locks. For instance, you can apply a straight-arm bar to take down your opponent. To enter, your lead hand can lop sao, or grab, your opponent's lead arm as your rear hand delivers a straight punch to the face. From there you can use your rear forearm to apply downward pressure on your opponent's lead arm to bring down your opponent. While he or she is on the ground, you can use your hand or your knee to continue to apply pressure on the arm. This straight-arm bar works well when your opponent's lead arm is stiff and resistant.

A figure 4 lock is another type of lock that can be applied when your opponent's arm is not stiff, but pliable. Basically, you bend your opponent's arm at the elbow and hold it in place with a wristlock. Your other hand is inserted inside the arm and grabs your wrist to maintain the lock. You can enter into the figure 4 lock from the lop sao and rear straight punch combination, bracing your opponent's elbow against your armpit. From there, you can bring your front leg behind his front leg and turn him so that he trips over your leg and falls onto his side.

While your opponent is on his side, you can maintain the figure 4 lock. While doing so, you put one leg in front of your opponent's face, while the other leg drops to the knee and is braced behind his back. You pull up on the locked arm. Then you can squeeze him by pushing forward with your rear knee while pulling back against his face with the back of your lower leg (see Figure 12-3).

Figure 12-3: Figure 4 lock takedown

The outside armpit lock is another useful lock that can be applied against your opponent's stiff lead arm. Again, you can apply this from the lop sao or grab your opponent's lead arm and simultaneous rear punch to the face. You then use your left armpit to press down on your opponent's arm as you pull the lead wrist upward, putting pressure on the elbow. You drop your opponent, face down, to the ground, and lean into him or her as you maintain the lock and apply pressure.

Strangleholds and Neck Chokes

There are various ways to strangle an opponent. In the front stranglehold you bring your opponent's head down in front of you, wrap your arm around his or her neck, and squeeze, using your other hand to assist your arm. One way to enter into the front stranglehold is to move from a pak sao, or front hand immobilization technique, to strike your opponent's face. While your opponent is stunned, you wrap your arm around the back of his or her neck and pull it down to execute the stranglehold. Another way to move into the front stranglehold is to slap the back of your opponent's neck with your front hand to pull the head forward. From there you can wrap your arm around the front of the neck and squeeze to complete the stranglehold.

In the top stranglehold, instead of being directly in front of your opponent, you are behind, looking over the back of your opponent's head as he or she is bent down. Your wrap your arm so that your forearm is in front of the neck. You use your other hand to hold your wrist as you pull up, squeezing the neck.

Figure 12-4: Rear stranglehold

In the side strangle you basically move to the side of your opponent to wrap your arms around his or her neck to squeeze. For instance, as your opponent lead punches, your rear hand parries the punch over your front shoulder, and your lead hand goes around the left side of your opponent's neck. You wrap your lead arm around the back of the neck, use your rear hand to grasp the wrist, and pull your arms together to apply the stranglehold.

The final type of stranglehold, the rear stranglehold, involves applying the technique to your opponent's neck as you are positioned behind him or her. To execute this strangle, you must insert your arm from behind and clamp it across the front of your opponent's neck. Make sure that the angle, or bend, of your elbow is braced directly in front of the windpipe. Your other arm rests on your opponent's shoulder, and you bend it so that your hand is braced at the back of his head (see Figure 12-4). You place your front hand on the bicep of your back arm. As you pull back with your front arm, your hand pushes your opponent's head forward. The countervailing forces result in a tight squeeze of your opponent's neck.

One way to enter into this position is to move off a pak sao, or front arm immobilization technique. As you trap the arm, you punch your opponent's face with your front hand and push his or her face to turn the head back. As the head turns, the rest of the body follows. This rotates your opponent's upper body so that the back of the head and neck are now available for you to apply the rear stranglehold.

Neck locks are similar to strangleholds. You do not merely choke your opponent, but clamp his or her neck in place. One example is a front face lock, in which you wrap your arm tightly around your opponent's face and pull upward as your other hand pushes your opponent's shoulder. Another example is the reverse figure 4 lock, in which you apply your outer forearm against your opponent's neck and brace your other hand against his or her shoulder.

Manipulations and Controls

Manipulations and controls represent a final category of grappling used in Jeet Kune Do. These involve maneuvering and controlling the various limbs of your opponent. One type is called the arm blast. You use this when your opponent reaches for you. Essentially you use both of your arms to push your opponent's arms downward so that your arms are on the inside. From there you can tackle your opponent or go into any number of different follow-ups.

Another type, the arm drag, is employed to pull your opponent's arm across his or her body, which allows you to maneuver to the outside of the arm. You basically grab your opponent's arm above the elbow and pull the arm forward so that your opponent goes past you.

The elbow throw-by is similar to the arm drag. It is used when your opponent tries to move his or her arm from outside your arm to the inside. As the opponent does so, you drop your arm to grab his or her elbow. You then throw your opponent's arm against his or her body, and you can shift into a follow-up position from there.

The elbow post involves pushing one or both of your opponent's arms upward. For example, you can apply this when your opponent is reaching for you. As you move your opponent's arms out of the way, you can shift in for a tackle or apply another grappling technique.

Grappling was an area that Bruce Lee researched and trained. Although he did not promote grappling as much as he did kickboxing and trapping, it became an integral part of his personal approach to combat. He found ways to take the existing knowledge from various systems and to make it flow from the various tools. Therefore, to understand the total art of Jeet Kune Do, one must study and learn the grappling skills that Lee believed were important to know.

Lee's Approach Foreshadowed Mixed Martial Arts

In his lifetime Lee already saw the need to integrate different martial arts elements into a total approach. In the early 1990s grapplers realized that they needed to know how to kick and punch, while stand-up martial artists realized they needed to learn how to grapple. The result is that many individuals today cross-train in stand-up arts and grappling.

part 4
the five ways of attack

N FORMULATING HIS ART of Jeet Kune Do, Bruce Lee realized that strictly passive defensive maneuvers were not the most efficient and effective ways to deal with an opponent. Rather, he concluded that offensive moves, which put the opponent on the defensive, produced better results. Therefore, Lee investigated ways to improve the offensive capabilities of his art and adapted some tactics from Western fencing into Jeet Kune Do. Known as the five ways of attack, they represent a compilation of all the possible methods of attack into a handful of categories.

In this and the next several chapters, we shall examine each of these ways of attack in detail. We will begin by looking at Single Direct/Angulated Attack, through which a person can successfully score with one technique in one move. Next, we will consider Attack by Combination, which allows a person to launch multiple techniques in sequence. Another approach, Progressive Indirect Attack, is a deceptive manner of attacking by using feints to set up an opponent. Attack by Drawing lulls an opponent into attacking by presenting an open target, then countering the opponent's move. Finally, Hand Immobilization Attack removes your opponent's defenses so that you can complete your attack.

chapter 13
single direct/
angulated attack

I F YOU TALK to some of the students who studied Jeet Kune Do directly with Bruce Lee, you will discover they all agree that he could easily hit an opponent with a single punch or kick. He had developed his speed, power, and ability to close the distance to such a high degree that he could reach an opponent at will. Lee had a strong intuitive sense of the right moment to make his move, when a person's mind was elsewhere and unprepared to deal with his attack.

Pete Jacobs, an original China-town student, recalls Lee's amazing speed when he first met him. He watched a fellow student continuously try to block Lee's single direct hit, without success. Even though Lee told him where he was going to strike him, the student could never stop him. This went on for about fifteen minutes.

SDA/SAA

These amazing feats that Lee's students personally witnessed are examples of Jeet Kune Do's Single Direct Attack (SDA). SDA represents the simplest manner of attacking an opponent. At the same time many factors must work together in order to make it effective. Moreover, it is the most challenging to master and to pull off successfully.

When employing SDA, a fighter executes only one technique, which is intended to land accurately on the target with the proper speed and power. A direct attack means that a person executes the technique in the most direct manner possible, usually along a straight path to the target. For example, a fighter employing SDA would execute a finger jab from the initial front hand position right to the opponent's eyes in a straight line.

A variation of SDA is known as Single Angulated Attack (SAA). In SAA the solo technique is fired from an angle—for example, while shifting slightly to the outside of an opponent's punch. The technique still moves along a direct path to the target, but does so from an angle because of different body positioning. To illustrate, suppose that an opponent, in unmatched lead, shoots a lead straight punch. You can step aside to move to the outside of the punch. As you do so, you fire your own lead punch, which slides across the opponent's arm into his face. Your shift in body positioning requires you to punch from an off-angle to the face.

There are certain elements that must work in harmony with each other, in order for either SDA or SAA to actually work. We examine these below:

- Distance: It almost goes without saying that you must be at the right distance relative to your opponent for your single strike to reach its intended target. If your opponent is too far from you, then your strike will fall short. If you are not within distance to reach your opponent, then you must use your footwork and mobility to close the gap so you can reach him or her. Alternately, you can wait until your opponent moves toward you and steps within range for you to strike.

- Timing: As stated before, one of the things that made Bruce Lee successful in SDA was his ability to know the right moment to launch his attack. Similarly, you must learn to recognize the appropriate time, when your opponent is most vulnerable to your single attack. There are certain moments when SDA will have a high probability of success.

Lee acknowledged the difficulty of successfully using simple attacks. Therefore, he encouraged attacking an opponent's lead leg or hand first. This would provoke a reaction on the part of the opponent and allow time to then pull off the simple attack.

For instance, when your opponent relaxes his or her guard and thereby exposes a specific target area, you can fire a punch, kick, knee strike, or elbow strike at that target area. If your opponent is distracted or thinking of something else, that offers a good opportunity to strike as well. Another time when it is appropriate to strike is when your opponent shifts position to execute a feint. You can land your strike at a target area that is exposed as a result. Also, you can strike when your opponent is in the midst of recovering after attacking you, because your opponent has not stabilized his or her position for an effective defense. Yet another opportune time to strike is when your opponent is preparing to attack, because his or her intention and hand movement are focused more on attack than on defense. In all these cases you need to develop a good, intuitive sense of the right moment to launch your attack.

- Speed: If you are too slow in executing your technique, you will never reach your intended target. Your opponent will have sufficient time to react and can defend in any number of different ways. To be successful, you must develop footwork speed, hand speed, and kicking speed to minimize the amount of time required to strike your opponent.

- Economy of Motion: In order to travel directly to the target, your limb must minimize the amount of movement needed to effectively execute the technique. Any unnecessary movement slows you down and consumes additional time. There should be no preparatory moves prior to executing the strike, such as a retraction of the hand or chambering of the leg. Such moves can telegraph your impending strike, giving your opponent a chance to defend against it. Therefore, you should work on refining your tools so that they are crisp and sharp.

- Defensive Coverage: While attacking, you should make sure that you are well covered against any counterattacks. Your strike may fall short or miss the target, allowing your opponent to counterstrike. If your rear hand is not positioned to protect against a probable attack, then you are vulnerable to being struck. So make sure that you have your hand up to protect your head and that your elbow is in place to protect your upper body.

SDA can be executed in a strictly offensive manner—for example, when you decide to advance toward your opponent at an opportune moment. You can also use SDA as a counteroffensive measure, for instance, when your opponent rushes at you and you launch a strike in response.

There are generally two effective means of accomplishing SDA. One is attacking from a state of immobility. This can work especially well after a series of feints and false attacks that lulls an opponent into expecting a more complex movement. The sudden and unannounced simple attack can catch your opponent completely off guard.

The other method is attacking from a variation of rhythm or cadence. For instance, you can change the rhythm and cadence by progressively slowing down your movements. Then, when your opponent has adjusted to your pace, you can launch a single strike at very high speed, catching your opponent unawares. Similarly, when opponents become set in tempo to your movements, a slight hesitation on your part can cause them to inadvertently open a way to your simple attack.

Examples of Single Direct Attack

Technically speaking, any lead or rear tool technique, whether it be a punch, kick, elbow strike, or knee strike, can be utilized for SDA. Even other tools, such as a forearm strike or a head butt, can be employed for SDA under the right circumstances. In his notes Bruce Lee identified certain specific tools that he believed represented good examples of SDA.

- Lead Shin/Knee Side Kick: All other things being equal, the shorter the distance between your tool and the target, the more quickly your tool will strike the target. This particular technique involves employing the longest weapon, your lead leg, to the nearest target, your opponent's front knee or shin. Because the distance between your front leg and your opponent's knee or shin is minimal, you can strike it very quickly.

    You can employ the lead shin/knee side kick in two basic ways. One is as an offensive action in which you strike your opponent when the moment presents itself. The other is as a counteroffensive move in which you strike when your opponent advances toward you or tries to attack you.

- Lead Finger Jab: This tool also makes use of short distances. It, too, employs the principle of using the longest weapon to the nearest target. In this case your longest hand weapon is your front hand with the fingers extended. The nearest targets are your opponent's

Figure 13-1: Finger jab

eyes. With the distance at a minimum, you can fire a lead finger jab at your opponent quickly with a relatively high probability of hitting the target (see Figure 13-1).

- Lead Jab: This tool uses your front fist to strike your opponent. Targets are typically the nose, chin, solar plexus, or midsection, all along the front of the body down the centerline. The lead jab is a very rapid, probing punch that is usually thrown suddenly, with great speed. It can strike without warning before an opponent has a chance to defend against it.

  The lead jab can be executed offensively, whether you are already in range to hit or you have to move into range to strike. If your opponent advances toward you, you can use the lead jab as a counteroffensive tactic.

- Lead Hook Punch: The lead hook punch propels your lead hand in a curving arc toward the side of your opponent's head. Some possible targets are your opponent's chin, jaw, and ear. It is an effective punch to use when your opponent is well guarded in front, making it difficult to deliver a straight-line punch.

  The lead hook punch is useful as an offensive technique, especially as a follow-up to another punch, such as a lead jab or a rear cross. It can also be employed as a counteroffensive technique, for example, against your opponent's rear cross.

In addition to these specific techniques that are contained in Lee's notes, there are other techniques that lend themselves well to SDA. These are as follows:

- Lead Snap Kick: This particular kick is useful to attack your opponent's groin. You lift your front knee up and snap your front foot directly to the target. There should be no chambering of the kick. Rather, your front foot should go in a straight line right to the groin.

  The lead snap kick can be applied offensively as an attack upon your opponent. You can also employ it as a counter against an opponent who tries to attack you.

- Lead Inverted Kick: This particular kick is used against an opponent who faces you in unmatched lead. As you lift up your front knee, you point it in the direction of the target. You then snap your front foot directly to the target, whether it is the groin, solar plexus, or even the head. Make sure that you do not chamber the kick but execute it in a straight line to the target.

You can throw the lead inverted kick as part of an offensive assault against your opponent. Alternately, you can use it as a counteroffensive move against an opponent who seeks to attack you.

- Lead Hook Kick: Like the lead hook punch, this kick is appropriate when you specifically want to hit the side of your opponent's body. Against an opponent in matched lead, you can aim for the front thigh, the groin, the ribs, or the side of the head. You lift the front knee, torque your body, turn your hips, and deliver the kick in a short, tight arc toward the target (see Figure 13-2). You should not chamber the kick or cock it back as you raise your leg, because such an action is neither economical nor direct.

Rather, you want to minimize the amount of time it takes for the foot to reach its target by flattening the path of the kick as much as possible.

The lead hook kick can be employed offensively, as when you advance to your opponent and target the thigh. It can also be used in a counteroffensive manner, for instance, against your opponent's ribs as he or she throws a rear cross.

Figure 13-2: Lead hook kick

Examples of Single Angular Attack

The main difference between the SDA and the SAA is that the latter is not delivered in a straightforward line. Rather, it is fired from an off-angle, usually as you position your body away from your opponent. The following are some examples of SAA using either punches or kicks.

- Lead Straight Punch: To execute this punch, you extend your front hand forward, rotating your hips and extending your lead shoulder so that your hand, arm, and both shoulders are aligned. Normally, your front hand will be in vertical fist position upon impact.

Nontelegraphing

The principle of not telegraphing your strikes is especially acute when it comes to SDA/SAA. If you telegraph your punch too much, for example, you will lose much of the surprise element of the punch. It will be as if you slowed down your punch, because it takes longer for the punch to reach its target once you have decided to execute it.

To deliver this punch in SAA fashion, you can step off to your right and fire the punch from that spot directly to your opponent's face. You may want to punch from an angle in order to take advantage of an opening or to surprise your opponent, who may be expecting a punch from the front.

This angulated punch can also be used as a counter against a rear cross or against a lead punch from someone in unmatched lead. As your opponent is about to fire one of these punches, you move laterally to your right to avoid the punch. You can fire the straight punch across your opponent's punch to help deflect it away from you. Your punch should strike your opponent at an angle.

- Lead Hook Kick: To deliver this in SAA fashion, you can move laterally to your left and fire the kick at your opponent. By stepping off, you are able to deliver your foot to targets that might be difficult to reach if you faced your opponent straight on. For instance, you can more easily land your kick on your opponent's front ribs because of your changed position.

  You can utilize the kick as part of an offensive maneuver in which you initiate the side step and then fire the kick at your opponent. You can also use this kick as a counter. For instance, if your opponent advances toward you, you can move laterally and fire the kick at his or her sternum.

Undoubtedly the proper cultivation of your fighting tools is essential if you are to achieve any success using SDA. You must learn the correct mechanics and form of each punch, kick, or other strike. You have to be able to strike the target accurately when it presents itself. Your strike must have sufficient power behind it to have an effect on your opponent. It must also be fired with great speed so that it lands before your opponent can react. Finally, you must make sure you are at the proper distance to reach your opponent. Correct footwork and mobility are needed to enable you to move into range. Practicing with a partner holding focus mitts or with a sparring partner helps greatly in developing these essential qualities.

The Hammer Principle

Bob Bremer, a student at the Chinatown school, teaches a way of implementing Simple Direct Attack through deception. Called the Hammer Principle, the idea is to lower your lead hand slightly, which brings it forward a few inches. Because it is closer to your opponent, you can strike him or her more quickly.

attack
by combination

BRUCE LEE extensively researched Western boxing, watching films of boxing matches and reading many books on the subject. He was so enamored by the "sweet science" that he incorporated a great deal of its footwork and its punching methodology into his Jeet Kune Do. Western boxers are taught how to punch in combination, that is, to throw multiple punches with one or both hands, usually to different targets. It is no surprise, therefore, that Lee grafted the concept of punching combinations from Western boxing onto his martial art. However, he expanded it to include kicking combinations and mixed hand and foot combinations. This approach became known as Attack by Combination (ABC).

ABC

In many cases a Single Direct Attack or Single Angulated Attack will not succeed in stopping an attacker. Your opponent may be too quick for you, able to easily defend against your single strikes. This is where a different approach, such as ABC, can prove very useful. ABC can be characterized as two or more strikes that flow in a natural sequence, usually to more than one target. So, even if your opponent can fend off your single attacks, it will be more difficult to consistently defend against multiple strikes delivered in this manner. In order to successfully use ABC, you must make several elements work in tandem with each other. These are as follows:

- Timing: In order to effectively apply ABC, you must attempt to land each strike at the appropriate moment, either when a selected target is already exposed or when your opponent exposes the target. Therefore, you have to pay careful attention to your opponent's responses to ensure that you do not land a strike in an area that is well covered or protected. Instead, watch to see how your opponent reacts and which areas of the body are left uncovered as a result of these reactions. That will guide you as to which strikes to implement.

For instance, if you throw a lead jab to the head and your opponent raises both arms to defend against it, you can follow up with a rear cross to the midsection, which is now exposed. As another illustration using a similar combination, suppose you throw a lead punch to the stomach. If your opponent drops his or her hand to try to parry it, you can then throw a rear cross to the chin, which is now exposed.

- Distance: In order for your strikes to score on your opponent, you must be at the proper distance for each of the specific techniques that you execute. While a kick can be thrown from a farther distance, an extended punch can only land if you are closer. Likewise, a knee or an elbow strike must be executed at close range in order to hit the target. Therefore, you must adjust your distance to facilitate the particular techniques that you are throwing. Moreover, you must be aware of any change in your opponent's position, whether it closes or opens the distance.

  For example, suppose that you move in from long range with a lead hook kick at your opponent's front thigh. After executing the kick, you can step down and fire a lead straight punch to your opponent's chin because you have bridged the gap into medium range. However, if your opponent retreats after your kick, he or she may be out of range for your lead straight punch. In that case you may want to follow up with a kick, which is capable of reaching your opponent.

- Speed: There are two kinds of speed that are of primary concern in ABC. One is the speed of each individual strike—that is, how quickly each strike can reach its intended target, known as movement speed. Each of the individual techniques that make up the combination must be thrown as quickly as you can to hit the target before your opponent has a chance to defend. Otherwise, you will find the target protected before you can reach it.

  The other kind of speed is combination speed, which refers to how quickly you can flow from one strike to the next in the sequence. You must not only land your initial strike at the intended target, but also land any subsequent strikes at the other targets before your opponent can react to them. If your combinations are thrown too slowly, your opponent may react quickly enough to counter each individual strike. Therefore, you must execute your strikes at a fast enough pace that your opponent cannot keep up.

At the same time, do not throw your combinations so quickly that you fail to take advantage of your opponent's reactions to individual strikes. For instance, if you merely blitz your opponent's head with multiple strikes while he or she keeps both arms up to protect it, you are neglecting the opportunity to attack any open areas. So regulate your speed in accordance with your opponent's reactions.

When a student starts to learn ABC, there is a tendency to execute the techniques too quickly, resulting in a loss of form and proper mechanics. Be sure that, as you learn different combinations, you execute each of the underlying techniques correctly. Otherwise, your combination will be sloppy.

- Accuracy: Each of the individual strikes that make up ABC must accurately hit the intended target in order to be effective. If you intend to kick your opponent's groin but miss and kick the thigh, you have not accomplished what you set out to do. Likewise, if try to punch your opponent's chin but end up striking only air, that punch has gone to waste.
- Natural Flow: Each strike must flow into the next strike in a smooth and unstilted manner. This facilitates speed, economy of motion, and directness. If you move from one technique to the next with awkward, clumsy, and unnatural pauses in-between, you will probably not land your strikes on their targets.

Also, the strikes must flow in a natural, logical sequence. For instance, a lead jab followed by a rear cross is a tried and true sequence. Likewise, a lead hook kick followed by a lead straight punch works well. However, a lead finger jab followed by a rear hook kick is rather awkward because you have to halt your motion after the finger jab to set yourself up to do the rear hook kick. Similarly, the combination of a lead backfist followed by a lead hook punch does not flow well because you must bring your fist all the way back to the other side to execute the hook punch.

Use of Feints and False Attacks in ABC

While you often will try to actually land each strike in ABC, sometimes you may wish to include feints and false attacks with strikes that are intended to score. You use the feints and false attacks as ways to set up your opponent for the final blow. The purpose of employing the feints and false attacks is to entice your opponent to respond in a way that exposes the real target area for your finishing strike.

For instance, you can feint both a jab and a rear cross to induce your opponent to parry with the rear hand. When the rear hand moves away from the side of your opponent's head, you strike that area with a lead hook punch. As another illustration, you can feint a jab to rear cross combination to draw your opponent's arms up. When the arms are raised, you can land a lead side kick to the midsection, which is exposed.

Use of Rhythm in ABC

To make your ABC even more effective, you can vary the rhythm of your strikes. In other words, rather than launch each strike in a uniform pattern of time, vary the speed of the individual strikes and the length of pauses between them. If you maintain a consistent, uniform pattern of timing in your combinations, your opponent can mimic your pattern and time each of your strikes. This will make it easy for him or her to defend against each of them. However, if you break the rhythm by slowing down or speeding up the strikes, as well as lengthening or shortening the pauses in-between, it will be more difficult for your opponent to time your hits. You will be able to insert your strikes in-between your opponent's motions, when areas are left exposed.

As a way to illustrate this principle, we will examine a few variations in the way you can execute a combination in which you start with a lead hook kick, followed by a lead finger jab, which is then followed by a rear cross. The speed of each individual strike will be designated either as "fast" or "slow." The length of time in-between strikes will be designated as either "long" or "short."

- Fast/Short/Fast/Short/Fast: In this example each strike is executed at top speed, with very little pause in-between. It is as if you are firing a machine gun at your opponent, because the strikes are coming one right after another. This is useful against an opponent who tries to keep up with you but is always one step behind.

- Fast/Long/Fast/Short/Fast: This time the only difference is that there is a longer pause between the lead hook kick and the lead finger jab. When you resume with the finger jab, everything moves in rapid, machine-gun fashion. The long pause between the lead hook punch and the lead finger jab can give you an opportunity to assess your opponent's reaction. If it is appropriate, you can then fire off the remaining strikes quickly.

- Fast/Short/Fast/Long/Slow: In this instance the lead hook kick and lead finger jab are thrown very quickly, with little pause. Then there is a pause before you throw the final strike, the rear cross. That punch is thrown at a slower speed. The idea here is that your opponent becomes conditioned to your first two strikes, which are delivered rapidly. Then, because your opponent expects the next strike to also be quick, he or she overreacts. You can then strike with the rear cross, taking advantage of your opponent's early reaction.

- Slow/Long/Slow/Long/Fast: In this example you throw your lead hook kick relatively slowly and pause before throwing the lead finger jab. Then, after a pause, you suddenly speed up in throwing the rear cross. The first two strikes basically lull your opponent into thinking you have a slow rhythm, and he or she is caught off guard when you spring the surprise of a quick rear cross.

- Slow/Long/Fast/Short/Fast: In this illustration your lead hook kick moves relatively slowly, and you pause. You suddenly fire a quick finger jab followed quickly by a rapid rear cross. The lead hook kick sets the pace by leading your opponent to think you are not that fast. You suddenly follow with two rapidly delivered strikes that catch your opponent unawares.

Examples of ABC

ABC can be categorized into four primary types: (1) hand to hand, (2) foot to foot, (3) hand to foot, and (4) foot to hand. In the following sections, we will examine examples of each.

Hand to Hand

This category of ABC refers to combinations in which hand strikes are thrown in logical, flowing combinations. Each of the hand strikes that make up these combinations can be launched with the intention of scoring. Alternately, you can throw the first one or two strikes as feints or false attacks, with only the final strike intended to land. The following are examples where each strike is intended to score.

• Lead Jab-Rear Cross: In this combination you can fire a lead jab to your opponent's nose, which should knock the head back slightly (see Figure 14-1). Then you follow up with a rear cross to the chin (see Figure 14-2), to knock your opponent backward, hopefully onto the ground. Another possibility is that you drop down and fire the rear cross at the

Figure 14-1: Lead jab

midsection to cause your opponent to bend over, giving you the opportunity for another follow-up strike. This is the classic combination known as the "one-two" in Western boxing.

• Lead Jab-Lead Hook Punch: In this example you fire a lead jab to your opponent's nose to knock back the head slightly. While your opponent is momentarily stunned, you can follow up with a lead hook punch to the side of the jaw, knocking him or her off to the side. Instead of throwing the lead hook punch to the head, you can throw it lower against your opponent's side. This combination is often referred to as the "one-three" in Western boxing.

• Lead Jab-Rear Cross-Lead Hook Punch: This combination is known as the "one-two-three" in Western boxing. After firing your lead jab at your opponent's face, you follow with a rear cross to the face. Then you finish with a

Figure 14-2: Followed by rear cross

lead hook punch to the jaw.

You can also fire the rear cross at the midsection instead of the face and follow with a lead hook punch to the body.

Watch any kind of Western boxing match, and you will see attack by combination being used frequently. The ones that you will see most commonly are double jab, jab-cross, and jab-hook. Combinations are the bread and butter of boxing at any level.

Foot to Foot

This category of ABC refers to combinations in which kicks are thrown in naturally flowing succession. In many cases you will launch each individual kick with the intent to strike a target. In other cases you may wish to set up your opponent with feints and false attacks and finish with a kick that is intended to score. The following examples illustrate combinations in which each kick is intended to land.

- Lead Snap Kick-Lead Snap Kick: In this combination, you throw a lead snap kick at your opponent's groin area. If your opponent retreats, you track him or her with your footwork and throw a second lead snap kick at the groin. The second snap kick should have more power behind it than the first one.

- Lead Snap Kick-Lead Hook Kick: This example shows how you can kick along one line and follow with a kick along a different line. You start with a lead snap kick to strike your opponent's groin area. If your opponent does not step back, you can follow with a lead hook kick to the ribs. If your opponent does step back, then your lead hook kick can be aimed at the thigh or knee. After the initial kick you can set your front foot down and spring up into the hook kick. Another option is to keep your front foot in midair immediately after striking the groin with the lead snap kick, then shift immediately into a lead hook kick without setting the foot down.

- Lead Hook Kick-Rear Hook Kick: This combination involves shifting from one foot to another in combination. You first fire a lead hook kick at your opponent, for example, at the lead thigh area. If your opponent then steps back into the opposite lead, you can throw a rear hook kick at the knee, thigh, groin, or other target area. The rear hook kick has a longer reach because your opponent has opened the distance by changing leads. Also, the change of leads means that your opponent's vulnerable targets have switched sides, so you switch your attacking tools to access those target areas.

Hand to Foot

This category of ABC involves following a hand strike with a kick. It generally requires you to move from a strike aimed at the upper body to a strike intended for the lower body of your opponent. Also, because the hands have a shorter reach then

Although most of the punching combinations in Jeet Kune Do are derived from Western boxing, one type that Lee carried over from Wing Chun is the jik chung chuie, or straight blast. This is a type of chain punch in which you deliver vertical fist punches down the centerline of the opponent.

the legs, it also means a shift in distance. The following are some examples of hand to foot combinations in which each strike is intended to score. Keep in mind that the hand strike can also be a feint or false attack, followed by a kick that actually lands.

- Lead Finger Jab-Lead Snap Kick: The lead finger jab is thrown while you are in, or as you enter, medium range and is aimed at your opponent's eyes. After the finger jab lands, if your opponent steps back, he or she will likely be out of range for another hand technique. You can then follow with a lead snap kick to the groin. This combination can be quite effective because your opponent's attention will be diverted to the eyes when you finger jab them, which opens up the groin for your kick.

- Lead Straight Punch-Lead Hook Kick: From medium range you launch the lead straight punch at the face, which knocks your opponent back. If he or she steps out of range for a follow-up punch, you can fire a lead hook kick to whatever target is available, which will most likely be somewhere in the lower body.

- Lead Backfist-Lead Side Kick: This time you throw the lead backfist against the face, which propels your opponent back. Assuming that your opponent steps so far back that you cannot follow with another hand technique, such as a rear cross, you can follow with a lead side kick. The kick can be directed to the midsection, the front knee, or the front thigh, depending upon which target is within range.

Foot to Hand

This final category of ABC refers to combinations in which you initially launch a kick at your opponent and follow up with a hand strike. This generally involves using the kick to move from long range into medium range where you can finish with the hand strike. It also involves shifting from a strike to the lower body of your opponent to a strike to the upper body. The following are some examples of foot to hand combinations in which each strike is intended to score. However, remember that the initial foot strike can also be a feint or false attack to set up your opponent for the finishing hand strike.

- Lead Snap Kick-Lead Finger Jab: You start by firing the lead snap kick to your opponent's groin. With your opponent's attention directed toward the lower body, you follow with a lead finger jab to the eyes. The kick takes you from long range into medium range, where you can reach your opponent with the finger jab. Both strikes are launched in a forward motion, and, therefore work well in combination.
- Lead Hook Kick-Lead Straight Punch: From long range you can advance toward your opponent with a lead hook kick, to the knee or thigh, for example. As soon as you land the kick, your front foot steps down, placing you in position for punching. You then follow with a lead straight punch to your opponent's face. The initial kick serves to bring your opponent's attention to the lower body, so that he or she is not focusing on defending the upper body against your hand strike.

Figure 14-3: Lead side kick to front knee

- Lead Side Kick-Lead Backfist: From long range you advance toward your opponent with a lead side kick aimed at the front knee (see Figure 14-3). After the kick lands, your front foot steps down. You follow with a lead backfist to your opponent's face (see Figure 14-4). The lead backfist is a logical choice for a hand strike because of the way the side of your body faces your opponent when you finish

Figure 14-4: Followed by lead backfist

the side kick. It would be diffi-cult to fire a straight punch or finger jab from that position.

Besides these primary cate-gories of ABC, you can throw combinations involving other tools, such as the knees and the elbows. Combinations can be composed of two, three, four, or even five or more tech-niques, depending upon the circumstances. When you take into account all the various striking tools, the different strikes, and the variations in rhythm that can be implemented, the number of combinations that you can do is virtually limitless. To focus on the basics, however, your combinations should be two or three strikes in sequence.

In order to develop proficiency in ABC, you must first establish a solid foundation in Single Direct Attack. The simple tools are the building blocks of ABC. If you are not executing your simple attacks with balance, coordination, speed, and power, you cannot expect to do ABC very well.

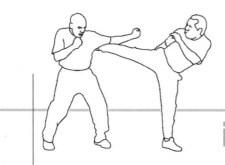

progressive
indirect attack

I N MANY FIELDS of endeavor, people rely on deception to help
them attain their objectives. In sports, such as basketball and
football, players sometimes pretend to pass the ball in one direction in order to throw off opposing players before they execute the actual,
intended play. During military conflicts, generals may send some troops to a
particular region to distract the enemy while transferring other troops to a
different region where they hope to surprise the enemy. The success or failure of such deceptive ploys depends upon the ability of the deceiver to lull the
opponent into believing and acting upon the false action.

Deception can play an important role in successfully dealing with an opponent in empty-hand combat. Bruce Lee realized this and incorporated the idea
of deception into Jeet Kune Do. It represents an integral part of Progressive
Indirect Attack (PIA), another one of the five ways of attack that make up
Lee's art.

As with other elements of Jeet Kune Do, Lee adapted the concept of PIA
from Western fencing. In the art of fencing, a player can deceive an opponent
by moving the foil along a certain line of attack to draw an anticipated
response from the opponent. When the opponent reacts in the expected way,
the player can suddenly change the timing and direction of the attack to strike
at a newly exposed target. For instance, a fencer can thrust the foil forward to
induce an opponent to do a downward parry. As the opponent does this, the
fencer quickly changes direction and thrusts the foil upward at the opponent's
face.

PIA operates in a similar way. You must first carefully note how your opponent responds to certain attacks that you aim at a particular target area. Your
observations will tell you how your opponent tends to react. More importantly, it will reveal the target areas that become vulnerable to a strike when

your opponent responds in that way. For example, you might observe that every time you throw a lead punch toward your opponent's midsection, the punch is parried with the front hand. Moreover, you notice that, when your opponent's hand drops to parry, it leaves the head exposed to a strike.

At a later point you can attack along the same line as before. This time, however, instead of completing the strike, you extend it only about halfway toward the target, just enough to make it appear that you are trying to attack that particular target. Because it seems that you are attempting to land the strike, your opponent responds in the same way as before. Then, while your opponent is in the process of reacting, you suddenly shift the line of your attack toward the target area that is exposed by the reaction to your false attack. Even if your opponent sees the change in your direction, your strike is way ahead of his or her ability to respond, so it succeeds it landing.

Using the same example as before, when you apply PIA, you throw your lead punch halfway toward your opponent's midsection. As the front hand moves down to parry your punch, you quickly redirect your punch upward to strike the face, which is now unprotected.

PIA is a viable option against an opponent who is difficult to hit when you try to use Single Direct Attack or Attack by Combination. Such an opponent may have evasive footwork or maintain a tight defense against SDA or ABC. Because this opponent tends to respond well to any attack you throw, the feint or false attack can be used to draw the same response so that you can score on a different line.

Components of PIA

Each word in "Progressive Indirect Attack" describes a specific element necessary for the attack to succeed. The word "progressive" means that you gain distance toward your opponent as you launch the false attack. If your opponent is out of your attack range, you must close the distance with your feint by at least half. Then, your second motion only has to cover the second half of the distance. As an example, if you throw a fake low punch to the midsection to set your opponent up for a lead punch to the face, you must step in deeply enough so that the lead punch will be able to reach the face.

"Indirect" means that you gain time on your opponent. You accomplish this by misdirecting your opponent's parry so that you can land the strike. Your movement should be ahead of your opponent's reaction, so that he or she is always moving in an opposite direction to the attack. As a result, your second movement—the actual attack—runs ahead of your opponent's parry, which is misdirected by your initial feint. Your actual attack should succeed in striking the target before your opponent has a chance to catch up to it.

Your initial feint or false attack must penetrate far enough and be held long enough to draw the opponent's parry. Your second movement, the actual attack, must be quick and decisive, not allowing your opponent a chance to recover.

The word "attack" means that you move ahead of your opponent's defensive responses so that you can land your intended strike. You should avoid allowing your opponent to make contact with your attacking limb. If he or she does so, your opponent can neutralize your attack, preventing you from scoring. By moving in the opposite direction from your opponent's reaction, you can successfully hit the target area with your final motion.

Certain other elements must be in place in order for PIA to succeed. If any of these elements are not operating at their maximum, your chances of executing PIA can diminish. Therefore in training for PIA, make sure that these elements are in play and working together.

- Distance: You must advance the proper distance as you throw the feint or false strike, so that you will close in on your opponent in preparation for your actual strike. You must also ensure that you are within range to hit your opponent when you implement your second movement, which is the intended strike. Always be mindful of how your opponent adjusts his or her own distance. If your opponent retreats when you make your initial feint or false attack, then you have to advance a longer distance to ensure that you can land your actual strike.

- Rhythm: In musical terms rhythm is a succession of beats within a specified period of time, or within a measure. For example, in a typical four-count measure, you have four evenly spaced beats that are counted as one, two, three, four. Rhythm plays a significant part in Jeet Kune Do in general and in PIA in particular. In order for PIA to work, you must stick to a specific rhythm, which involves actually hitting on the half-beat.

  In an evenly timed attack combination, your first strike would be considered the first beat, your second strike the second beat, and so on. If your opponent successfully parried each of those strikes, then none of them would land. In PIA your initial feint or false attack, as well as your opponent's attempt to parry, is considered the first beat. You speed up your second movement to land ahead of your opponent's next reaction. In other words, you hit in-between the first and second beats—that is, on the half-beat.

- Timing: To make PIA work, you must time your movements in accordance with your opponent's reactions. If you try to hit your opponent with your intended strike before your opponent has

> **A**ccording to Lee, surprise is a necessary part of PIA. You must avoid any hesitation, motion, or telegraphing that might alert your opponent of your intentions. You do not want your opponent to successfully defend against your attack.

even tried to parry your feint or false attack, you may find that the target area is still closed. This results either from initiating the feint or false attack too quickly or from not holding it long enough to give your opponent the chance to react.

On the other hand, if you are too slow with your movements, then your opponent can keep up with you. In that case you will also find that, when you try to hit your opponent, the intended target area is closed. Because your movements are too slow, your opponent is able to react to them in time, and you are unable to land your strike.

- Economy of Motion: Each of your motions must be delivered with minimal movement. There should be no retraction of your limb after executing the feint or false attack, prior to the launch of your actual strike. If the same limb delivers both the feint or false attack and the actual strike, then the intended strike should start from where your feint or false attack ended. For instance, if you fake a low lead punch at your opponent, your lead arm should move forward half the distance. If you intend to strike with a lead backfist, then that technique should cover the remaining distance without first retracting your lead arm.

Similarly, if one limb launches the feint or false attack, and a different limb delivers the actual strike, the limb executing the feint or false attack should not retract before you begin delivering the intended strike with the other limb. For example, if you fake a lead finger jab at your opponent's head and follow with a lead hook kick, you should not retract the lead hand before launching the kick.

- Deception: For PIA to work, your opponent must actually respond to your initial feint or false attack. You have to effectively sell your feint or false attack to persuade your opponent that the strike is real, so that he or she parries in the desired manner. Otherwise, the intended target area for your actual strike will remain covered. Therefore, you must make sure that your initial fake or false attack is thrown far enough and with body language that will convince your opponent that you are executing a real strike.

Categories of PIA

PIA can be classified in terms of outside lines, inside lines, high, middle, low, front, and rear. Each category contains numerous techniques that you can use, depending upon how your opponent responds. These are as follows:

- Inside to Outside: This type of PIA involves throwing a feint or false attack along an inside path toward your opponent to draw his or her hand away from an outside target area. As you draw the parry, you suddenly shift to strike your opponent at the outside target. For example, you fake a lead punch toward the face to draw a rear parry. When your opponent's hand moves to protect against the lead punch, you shift to a lead hook punch to the side of the head, which is now exposed.

- Outside to Inside: In this category of PIA, you begin by faking a strike along an outside line to draw your opponent's parry. When he or she responds, you switch to a strike on an inside path to hit a target that is now exposed. To illustrate, suppose that you fake a lead hook kick to your opponent's side to draw the rear arm down to cover. When your opponent responds, the head is left open, and you can finish with a lead finger jab to the eyes.

- High to Middle: You can fake a strike along the high line toward your opponent's head to draw a reaction. As your opponent moves one or both arms up to protect against that strike, you can suddenly shift to a strike to the midsection, which has become vulnerable. For instance, you can fire a lead finger jab toward the eyes, which causes your opponent to raise both arms for protection. As the arms move away, you shift to a lead punch to the sternum, which is now exposed.

- Middle to High: In this situation you fire a strike toward the middle of your opponent's body. When this draws your opponent's hand down, you shift to a high-line strike at the now exposed face. For example, you execute a lead punch to your opponent's midsection, which draws a front-hand parry. As the front hand moves down, you shift to a lead backfist to the face, which is now exposed.

- High to Low: This category involves firing a fake high-line strike to the face to draw your opponent's arm or arms up. With your opponent's attention focused on protecting his or her head, the lower body is vulnerable, so you follow with an actual kick to a low-line target. To illustrate, suppose that you fire a lead straight punch toward your opponent's head. As the arms move up to protect the head, you can follow with a front snap kick to the groin, which is now vulnerable.

- Low to High: In this type of PIA, you throw a low-line kick to draw a downward parry. When your opponent reacts in the expected way, you suddenly shift to a high-line hand strike. For instance, you can fake a front snap kick to your opponent's groin, which your opponent seeks to protect by lowering the front hand. This exposes the head for a lead straight punch to the face as your actual intended strike.

- Front to Rear: For this category you fake a strike with a lead limb to draw your opponent's parry. As your opponent responds, you follow with a rear strike to the newly exposed target area. For example, you can fire a fake lead hook punch to the head, which draws your opponent's rear hand outward to block or cover the side of the head. This can expose the face to your rear cross, your intended strike.

- Rear to Front: In this situation you fake a rear strike to draw your opponent's parry. When he or she responds accordingly, you throw an actual strike with a lead limb to the target area that becomes exposed. To illustrate, suppose you fake a rear cross to which your opponent responds with a rear-hand parry. Because the rear hand has moved away from the side of the head, you can follow with a lead hand hook punch along the outside line to the head.

In addition to these, there are other ways to classify PIA that can prove useful in learning and memorizing this type of attack. These broad categories have to do with the specific tools that are used and the order in which they are employed. Some specific examples of each of these are as follows:

- Hand to Hand: This category covers all the various types of PIA involving a fake hand strike followed by an actual hand strike.
    - Fake lead punch to the midsection to actual lead hooking palm strike to the head: In this example you execute a fake lead punch toward your opponent's midsection to draw a rear-hand downward parry

(see Figure 15-1). This action exposes the side of your opponent's head to an attack. You shift to a lead hooking palm strike to that target area, shown in Figure 15-2.

- Fake lead backfist to head to rear cross to midsection: In this particular sequence you fake a lead backfist to draw your opponent's upward front-arm block. This response exposes the midsection for your actual strike, a rear cross.

- Fake lead uppercut to rear cross to head: In this example you begin by faking a lead uppercut to your opponent's chin. This draws the front hand down to protect the chin, exposing the face. You follow with an actual rear cross to the head.

Figure 15-1: Fake low punch to draw rear hand down

- Foot to Foot: This category covers a myriad of situations in which you first throw a fake foot strike to draw a reaction from your opponent. You then follow with an actual foot strike to the newly exposed target area.

  - Fake front snap kick to lead hook kick: In this example you first fake a front snap kick to your opponent's groin area to draw your opponent's rear-hand downward parry. With the rear hand occupied, there is nothing protecting your opponent's left rib area. You follow with a lead hook kick to your opponent's ribs.

Figure 15-2: Followed by hooking palm strike to head

- Fake lead inverted kick to lead shin kick: Your opponent faces you in mismatched lead. You fake a lead inverted kick to the groin area, which draws a front-hand downward parry to protect the groin. You then shift to a lead kick to the front shin, which has become vulnerable as a result.

- Fake lead hook kick to middle to high lead hook kick: You begin by faking a lead hook kick to the middle of your opponent's body, to draw a rear-arm parry. The lowered arms leave the side of the head exposed. You follow with a high lead hook kick to the head.

> ## PIA in the Movies
>
> In *The Return of the Dragon*, Lee uses PIA against Bob Wall during one of their fights. After using a front snap kick twice against Wall, which draws his front-hand parry, Lee fakes the next kick and switches to a high lead hook kick to Wall's head.

- **Hand to Foot:** This classification covers the many situations in which you fake a hand strike to the high-line area, in order to draw an upward response by your opponent. This leaves the lower body vulnerable to a lead kick as an actual strike.

  - Fake lead finger jab to lead hook kick: In this example you fake the lead finger jab toward your opponent's eyes. Your opponent's arms move up to protect against the finger jab (see Figure 15-3), thereby exposing the lower body. You then follow with a lead hook kick to the thigh, shown in Figure 15-4.

  - Fake lead straight punch to lead side kick: In this instance you fake the lead straight punch high toward your opponent's face. As your opponent raises both arms to protect the face,

Figure 15-3: Fake lead finger jab to draw hands up

Figure 15-4: Followed by lead hook kick

the midsection is exposed. You follow with a lead side kick to your opponent's midsection.

- Fake lead backfist to lead inverted kick: In this situation your opponent is in mismatched lead. You fake a lead backfist to your opponent's face to draw the arms up. This response exposes the groin area to your actual strike, a lead inverted kick.

- Foot to Hand: This type of PIA employs a fake kick to draw your opponent's parry downward. You follow with an actual hand strike that lands on an upper-body target.
    - Fake lead hook kick to lead straight punch: This example involves faking the lead hook kick to draw your opponent's downward front parry. When your opponent reacts in this way, it exposes his or her face to an actual strike. You follow by executing a lead straight punch to the face.
    - Fake lead side kick to lead backfist: In this instance you lift your front knee as if to execute a lead side kick. When your opponent's front hand drops to parry, you launch a lead backfist to the face, which is now exposed.
    - Fake lead inverted kick to lead backfist: This situation involves your opponent facing you in mismatched lead. You fake a lead inverted kick to the groin area, which draws your opponent's front hand down to parry the kick. With the face now exposed, you follow with a lead backfist to that target area.

When used judiciously, PIA can be a very powerful and effective tactic for attacking your opponent. It can be the best strategy against an opponent who defends well against other types of attacks, such as Single Direct Attack and Attack by Combination. In PIA you are able to take advantage of the quickness of your opponent's responses to your strikes. In reacting to your attack, your opponent must move his or her hand from one area to another, which exposes an area for your actual attack.

"I've added in a progressive indirect attack to the original chi sao, which is close-quarter combat. Progressive indirect attack is the link to achieve chi sao. Progressive indirect attack is used against an opponent whose defense is tight and fast enough to deal with simple attacks like straight blast, finger jab, pak sao, and hit." (Lee 1997, p. 115)

More PIA in the Movies

In *Game of Death*, Lee has a famous *nunchaku* fight with the Escrima master played by his student Dan Inosanto. At one point Lee fakes a downward strike with the weapon, which draws Inosanto's downward block. Lee then executes a lead hook kick to Inosanto's head. This is another example of PIA.

attack by drawing

I F YOU WANTED TO CATCH A MOUSE in a building, one way might be to search around for it. However, the mouse could prove to be quite elusive. It might take hours, if not days, to track it down in order to capture it. A more successful approach might be to place several mousetraps, baited with food, throughout the building. Instead of actively looking for the rodent, you would, in effect, draw it out by attracting it to the mousetrap. Once the mouse made contact with the trap, it would be caught.

In combat sometimes the best way to deal with opponents is to lure them into traps where you can strike them when they are vulnerable. Rather than try to attack in a manner that may not succeed, you bait your opponent into attacking you. Doing that will necessarily expose some part of the body that you can then counterattack. In Jeet Kune Do this is known as Attack by Drawing (ABD).

ABD is sort of a cousin to Progressive Indirect Attack (PIA). Both of them require the use of deception to induce your opponent to react in a certain way, in order to expose a target area for your strike. However, they approach the problem differently. In PIA you launch a feint or false attack to deceive your opponent into believing that you are executing a real attack. Your opponent takes some type of defensive action, such as parrying with the hand, in response to the perceived attack. The parrying hand necessarily moves away from another part of his body. You then execute an actual strike on this newly exposed target area.

In ABD, rather than induce your opponent to take a defensive action, you lure him or her into committing an offensive action, for example, a punch or a kick. Taking such an action exposes some part of the body, and you then counterattack this newly exposed target area.

ABD can be used against all kinds of opponents. However, it may be the best option against an opponent who does not like to initiate a strike, but rather waits for you to attack first and then counterattacks. By applying ABD you can induce your opponent to attack by presenting what appears to be an opportunity for a strike against you. In some instances you can take an offensive action that your opponent tries to counter. You then counter the counterattack.

Elements of ABD

As in other ways of attack in Jeet Kune Do, there are certain elements that must operate in harmony if you want to successfully use ABD. These are as follows.

- Deception: This is a crucial part of ABD. You must take an action that effectively deceives your opponent into believing that he or she she must attack you in some way. You must make it appear that an action has to be taken immediately in response to your move. For example, if you want your opponent to throw a lead hook punch so that you can counter with a rear cross, you must make it appear that a target area has become available for a strike with a lead hook punch. You can do this by lowering your rear hand, for instance, so that it looks as if the side of your head is unprotected.

    In addition to taking the appropriate action, you must do it in a subtle way so that your opponent thinks you have committed an error. If your opponent suspects that you are setting a trap, he or she will avoid taking the bait and will not offer you the response that you want.

If you find that your training partners are not taking your bait, you might ask them if your baiting actions are too obvious. They will not fall for your invitation if they realize that you are simply trying to draw them into your trap. Your training partners should provide you with valuable feedback to help you improve.

- Speed: In launching your counterattack against your opponent's attack, you must generate enough speed to be able hit your opponent at the right moment. You may be successful in luring your opponent to attack you in the way you desire, but if you cannot strike the exposed target area quickly enough, before your opponent retracts, you may well find it covered. As an example, suppose again that you lower your rear hand to draw a lead hook punch. When your opponent starts to throw the punch, if you are unable to throw your rear cross fast enough to your opponent's face, he or she she may be able to retract the lead arm into a position where it can protect the face from you. Therefore, when the window of opportunity is available for you to counterattack, you must do so rapidly, before the window closes.

- Timing: This is another critical element that must be present for ABD to operate properly. When you induce your opponent to attack, you must employ your counterstrike at just the right moment, when the target area becomes exposed. If you attempt to counterstrike too early, before your opponent has reacted sufficiently to your action, you may find the target area still closed. For instance, if you lower your rear hand and try to throw a rear cross before your opponent attempts to attack you with a lead hook punch, you may find that your opponent's face is still protected by the front hand.

    Similarly, if you launch your counterstrike too late, after your opponent has fired an attack in response to your action, you may also find that your intended target is no longer exposed. For example, if your opponent has thrown a lead hook punch, and you start to launch your rear cross as he or she she is retracting the lead arm, you may find that you cannot get through to strike the face.

- Distance: A final element that must be in place for ABD to work is proper distance. You must be at the right distance relative to your opponent in order to land your counterstrike. If you fire your strike when your opponent is too far away, it will not reach the appropriate target. If you throw your strike when you are too close, you may end up jammed.

    Distance is also important in terms of your opponent's attack. On the one hand, if you are too far away when you try to draw an attack, your opponent may not take the bait because he or she she perceives that the strike cannot reach you. On the other hand, if you are too close to your opponent when you try to draw a strike, the attack can reach you more quickly. Your opponent may end up striking you before you have a chance to counterattack.

Types of ABD

There are basically three types of ABD that you can employ:

- You can use a defensive approach, in which you subtly but deliberately expose a target area of your body. This is to mislead your opponent into thinking that there is an opportunity to strike you there. Then, when your opponent takes the bait by directing a punch or kick at that area, you counterattack that part of his or her body that becomes exposed as a result.

- An offensive approach to ABD could involve you attacking your opponent's defense by means of a hand immobilization attack, for example. To use this approach, you could trap your opponent's lead arm to draw a countering rear punch. You would then parry the punch with your lead hand and strike with your own rear punch.

- A third approach to ABD, also offensive, is to draw a response by using feints or false attacks. Once your opponent reacts to your feint by attacking, you counter with your own strike to your opponent's exposed target area.

Lee's student Ted Wong likes to hold his front hand slightly lower than most Jeet Kune Do practitioners. By doing so, he lulls his opponent into thinking that his upper body is exposed. Then, when his opponent takes the bait and moves in, Wong intercepts with a lead straight punch.

Offensive ABD is a way to force your opponent to counterattack you, especially if he or she does not react to your invitations to attack. Think of a SWAT team trying to get a suspect out of a barricaded house. If they cannot lure him out, they can fire gas pellets to compel him to come out.

Examples of ABD

The following are some examples of ABD that you can initiate defensively.

- Lower Rear Guard to Lead Straight Punch: You first lower your rear guard to mislead your opponent into believing that the side of your head is unprotected (see Figure 16-1). If he or she takes the bait, your opponent may throw a lead hook punch in an attempt to strike the side of your

Figure 16-1: Lower rear hand to draw lead hook punch

Figure 16-2: Counter with lead straight punch

head. When the punch starts, you rapidly fire a lead straight punch to the face, which is left exposed when your opponent's front arm is extended (see Figure 16-2).

- Lower Rear Guard to Rear Cross: In this situation, when you lower your rear guard and your opponent throws a lead hook punch, you rapidly fire a rear cross at your opponent's now unprotected face.
- Variation: Instead of a lead hook punch, your opponent may throw a high lead hook kick toward your head. If you draw this reaction, you can drop down and counter with a rear cross to the groin area.
- Lower Front Hand to Lead Side Kick: In this instance you subtly lower your front hand to deceive your opponent into thinking that your face is exposed to a lead punch. As he or she starts to fire the lead punch, you lean your upper body back and counter with a lead side kick to the shin.
- Lower Front Hand to Lead Hook Kick: This time your opponent faces you in unmatched lead. When you lower your front hand, he or she starts to throw a lead jab at your head, which appears exposed. You sway back and counter with a lead hook kick to your opponent's ribs. The fact that your opponent is in opposite lead makes this target area more readily available for your kick.
- Lower Front Hand to Lead Straight Punch: In this case you subtly lower your front hand to lure your opponent to advance toward you, perhaps

with a lead punch. As your opponent moves into range, you quickly fire a lead straight punch to the face. This will work well if your opponent's guard is down or relaxed as he or she rushes toward you.

- Raise Rear Guard to Rear Hook Kick: In this situation you raise your rear guard hand to expose the rear side of your ribs. If your opponent responds by firing a lead hook kick toward your ribs, you can counter with a rear hook kick to his or her support leg. You must make sure your rear leg is far enough below your opponent's lead leg when you kick.
- Raise Lead Guard to Lead Hook Kick: This time you lift your lead guard to expose the front side of your ribs. If your opponent takes the bait and throws a rear hook kick toward your ribs (see Figure 16-3), you can counter by firing a lead hook kick to the support leg, as shown in Figure 16-4.

Figure 16-3: Raise lead hand to draw rear hook kick   Figure 16-4: Counter with lead hook kick to support leg

- Retreat to Lead Intercepting Kick: You can use your footwork to move back in order to lure your opponent to throw a rear step-through kick. As the kick is thrown, you counter with a lead side kick to the shin to stop the movement, as well as to hurt your opponent's leg.

The following are examples of ABD that you can initiate offensively, either by attacking your opponent's defense and forcing a reactive attack, or by using feints and false attacks to invite an attack.

- Trap to Rear Punch: You can execute a pak sao trap of your opponent's front arm along with a lead straight punch to induce your opponent to counter with a rear punch. As your opponent starts to throw the punch, you pick it up with a front-arm block that dissolves the punch. As you do so, you fire your own rear straight punch at your opponent's face.

- Trap to Lead Bridging Punch: This time you use a jut sao jerking hand trap of your opponent's front arm with your rear hand. As your opponent counters with a rear cross, you shift to your right and counter with a lead straight punch that bridges across your opponent's arm, striking the face.
- Feint to Lead Hook Punch: In this instance you feint a low rear cross to induce your opponent to counter with a lead hook punch to your head. As he or she does so, you go under the punch with a bob and weave. While you are moving underneath your opponent's arm, you counter with a lead hook punch to the midsection.

Like Progressive Indirect Attack, Attack by Drawing operates by deceiving an opponent into committing to a specific action—in this case, an attack. When the opponent takes the bait, a target is exposed to your counterattack. This method can be particularly useful against an opponent who does not like to initiate a strike, but who can be lulled into attacking. It is a viable option that the Jeet Kune Do fighter should train and have available when the need arises.

Understand that, in using ABD defensively, you have to make deliberate errors to expose yourself to attack so that you can counterattack. Ironically, your instructor now wants you to intentionally make mistakes—lowering your lead or rear hand, for example—that you were previously told to avoid.

hand immobilization
attack

OF THE FIVE WAYS of attack, perhaps none generates more controversy among modern-day Jeet Kune Do practitioners than Hand Immobilization Attack (HIA). This way of attack is based upon the deployment of trapping hands, which Bruce Lee modified and adapted from the classical gung fu art, Wing Chun. Some Jeet Kune Do practitioners do not train or teach HIA because they do not believe in its effectiveness against street fighters and contemporary martial artists. While they may acknowledge that one can become a decent trapper with enough time and experience, they believe that there are other methods that can help a student become proficient at close range more quickly and more effectively. Others continue to believe in the efficiency of the trapping methods employed in Lee's original art. They study it, practice it, become proficient at it, and pass it on to their students. Still others accept a compromise between the two positions, holding to the basic concept of trapping, but in forms different from those taught by Lee.

Wing Chun Hidden in Jeet Kune Do?

Patrick Strong, a student at Lee's Seattle school, thinks that Lee never abandoned the Wing Chun structure, as many believe. Instead, he argues that the Wing Chun structure is still there, although it is not as obvious. According to Strong, it is this structure that some JKD practitioners are missing from their art.

Whatever one may believe about the usefulness of trapping, one thing is certain: HIA is definitely an integral part of Jeet Kune Do, as practiced and taught during Lee's lifetime. Therefore, to learn and understand Jeet Kune Do completely, as well as to pass it on to future generations, a student must study the methods associated with HIA. This is not merely for historical reasons, either. As we shall see, trapping can be very effective against certain opponents under the right circumstances.

The Historical Origins of HIA

A brief historical review is useful in helping the Jeet Kune Do student understand the roots of the trapping hands technique and the reasons for its prominent place in the evolution in Jeet Kune Do. When Bruce Lee was growing up in Hong Kong, he began to study the art of Wing Chun at a school operated by Yip Man, the head of the system at that time. While its forms were not fancy or elegant, Lee liked the high value it placed on practical combat.

Wing Chun is largely a close-quarters system that emphasizes fighting through the sense of touch. Unlike other gung fu systems that stress striking from a nontouching position, Wing Chun teaches students to attach their arms to their opponents' arms. This allows students to feel the energy of their opponents' movements and thereby read their opponents' intentions. By being aware, through touch, of what an opponent is doing, a student can trap, or immobilize, the opponent's arms.

Trapping the opponent's arms accomplishes several objectives. First, you can remove a barrier that might prevent you from striking. Second, you prevent your opponent from using the trapped arm to strike you. Third, it enables you to more easily control your opponent.

Lee studied Wing Chun diligently for several years. He became so proficient at it that he became part of a small band of Wing Chun practitioners who fought other gung fu stylists. Although Lee did not complete the entire curriculum by the time he left Hong Kong for the United States, he attained a high level of skill in the art.

After arriving the United States, Lee continued to practice Wing Chun. During the first few years, the martial arts that he taught were a mixture of some of the Wing Chun trapping and other gung fu methods that he had picked up. Over time, he modified the trapping, so that it was no longer Wing Chun in its pure form as he had learned it. However, this new hybrid, which he called Jun Fan, his Chinese name, maintained trapping as its core.

As Lee continued to change his art, adding Western boxing, medium-range kicks, and fencing principles, trapping remained an essential part of the art, although no longer the primary focus. Nevertheless, HIA was still important enough to take its place as one of the five ways of attack in Jeet Kune Do. The curricula at his three schools in Seattle, Oakland, and Los Angeles all included basic trapping methods. However, Lee's version of trapping assumed a more aggressive nature than in Wing Chun, largely as a follow-up to kicks and punches.

During the latter part of the 1960s and through the early 1970s, Lee himself no longer employed trapping as much in his training. Although he did not abandon it, he greatly de-emphasized it because he found that he no longer needed to use it. Lee became so adept in closing the distance and in other fighting methods that it became unnecessary for him to employ trapping techniques. In fact, at one point he told Taky Kimura, his assistant instructor in charge of the Seattle group, that *chi sao*, a sensitivity exercise from Wing Chun, was "out."

Since Lee's passing, his students have preserved the trapping aspects of Jeet Kune Do. While some have trained more and some less, the first generation of Jeet Kune Do practitioners and their students are making diligent efforts to ensure that current practitioners can learn, appreciate, and use HIA.

Elements of HIA

The Jeet Kune Do fighter's objective is to hit the opponent. Generally, it is only when your opponent puts up a barrier or obstacle—such as a front-arm block to prevent you from striking—that trapping comes into play. The purpose of trapping, at that point, is to remove the obstacle so that you can continue your strike. In most cases trapping does not occur because you seek it. Rather, it occurs accidentally or incidentally, as you try to hit your opponent. So trapping is not an end in itself, but rather a means to an end, namely hitting.

There are certain elements that must be in place in order for HIA to work. These are as follows:

- Structure: Your opponent must present an appropriate fighting structure in which you can execute a trap. This means that your opponent places his or her arms in certain positions that prevent you from striking. For instance, in many styles an opponent has one hand in front and the other hand near the back. When he or she uses either arm to block or parry your punch, you can trap that arm and then strike.

  Certain fighting styles do not have the right type of structure for you to execute a trap. For example, Muay Thai fighters tend to put their arms up and wide apart. Their arm positions do not lend themselves to the type of trapping used in Jeet Kune Do. Certain types of wrestlers and grapplers like to crouch down and keep their hands low. This style also does not present an appropriate structure for trapping. So you have to evaluate the suitability of HIA according to the type of opponent you are facing.

In addition, your own structure must be proper for trapping. HIA takes place at close range, where your lead or rear hand can reach your opponent's arm in order to immobilize it. Your rear shoulder should be more forward, so that your upper torso is more squared up as it faces your opponent. This resembles the classical Wing Chun stance in which both your shoulders are forward. This position enables you to have two "guns," namely your front hand and your rear hand, available for striking. You also lean your upper body back just slightly for added safety from an opponent's counterstrike. However, the lower half of your body remains in basic bai-jong position, with your lead leg in front and rear leg in the back. This gives you the proper grounding from which to punch and also allows you to continue to use your footwork to move around.

- Distance: In order to trap your opponent's arm and to strike your target, you must be within the right range. You need to be close enough so that your trapping hand is able to reach your opponent's arm to immobilize it. Also, while trapping, you must be able to reach your opponent with your punch without leaning forward and breaking your balance.

  If you trap from too far away, you may be able to remove your opponent's arm from the path of your punch to some extent, but your punch will fall short of its target. You may be tempted to overreach with your punch, which will subject you to being grabbed by your opponent and pulled off-balance. If you trap from too close, however, you may end up getting jammed and unable to strike with much power. Your opponent might be able to smother your trap, rendering it ineffective.

- Response: For HIA to work at all, your opponent must give you the right response. Usually this means an attempt to block or parry your punch. To resume your punch, you will have to move the arm that is blocking its path. If your opponent does not manage to parry or block your punch, then you do not need to trap, unless you are attempting to trap preemptively.

For you to implement a specific trap, your opponent must give you the appropriate response to call forth that trap. For instance, for a pak sao, or slap hand, your opponent's front arm has to block your lead punch. If your opponent does not respond in the proper manner, then you have to switch to a different trap or a different technique. For example, if your opponent uses the rear arm, instead of the front arm, to block your punch, you use a *lin lop sao*, or grab hand, and strike your opponent with a lead backfist.

- Speed: When you try to punch and encounter a block or a parry, you have only a fraction of a second in which to trap your opponent's arm. If you fail to do so within that time, your opponent may disengage the arm from you. Worse yet, that same arm may be used to attack you. So you must trap very quickly before your opponent can counter.

   While the trap is applied, your punch must continue from that point at a high rate of speed. Your objective was, and continues to be, to hit. Therefore, as soon as you remove the barrier, your punch should explode toward your opponent as quickly as possible.

- Timing: This is another important aspect of HIA. You must time your trap to occur precisely when your punch runs into a barrier. This represents a very brief moment when your opponent is vulnerable to being trapped. If you try to do HIA too early before your opponent gives you an appropriate response, you may fail to trap because you have not yet encountered a barrier. On the other hand, if you do HIA too late, your opponent may counterattack by disengaging his or her arm or by trapping you instead.

- Pressure: HIA is a very aggressive type of attack in which you try to disrupt your opponent's balance, energy, and attitude. Therefore, when you trap and punch, you should generally apply forward pressure upon your opponent. At the moment that your punch runs into your opponent's block or parry, your punching energy should not stop and then resume when the arm has been trapped—rather, at the point of contact with the barrier, your front hand and arm should continue to press forward toward the target. In that way, when you remove the barrier of your opponent's arm, your punch should immediately take off. Think of water building up in a hose and then bursting forth when you finally open the nozzle.

- Sensitivity: This is the final element that you must have in order to make HIA work. In a moment's time you have to become aware of what your opponent is doing, so that you can automatically execute the right trap. For example, suppose your opponent uses a front-arm block to parry your lead punch. If the front-arm energy is rather loose, you can trap the arm with a pak sao to remove it from the path of your punch.

However, if your opponent's front-arm energy is rather stiff, you will find it difficult to trap the arm through a pak sao. Instead, your front hand can disengage from the front arm as your rear hand moves up to cover it. Your front hand can execute a jao sao, or running hand, strike to the side of your opponent's head.

But if your opponent's front-arm energy is moving forward toward you, then you can utilize a lop sao, in which you grab and pull your opponent's arm toward you while punching with your rear tool.

Sensitivity Drills

To help students develop their tactile awareness—that is, an ability to feel and read their opponents' intentions—Jeet Kune Do utilizes sensitivity drills. These exercises were taken from classical gung fu systems, primarily Wing Chun and praying mantis. When practicing these drills, two students work with each other. They present specific hand and arm positions to each other, and project certain energies, to train their capacity to respond in an appropriate manner. While it is difficult, if not impossible, to fully understand the drills merely by reading about them, the following descriptions can provide an idea of the types of drills that are used.

- *Don Chi Sao*: This drill was taken from the Wing Chun system. Each partner utilizes one arm that remains in contact with the other's opposing arm. For example, if your partner is using the right arm, you touch with your left arm. The partners take turns, each engaging in a set sequence of moves to which the other must respond using different types of energy.
- Chi Sao: Also from the Wing Chun system, this drill requires each partner to keep both arms in contact with the other's arms. The partners roll their arms from one position to the next, as if turning a steering wheel. They apply forward pressure and try to retain the structural integrity of their positions to prevent each other from striking. They can practice switching hand positions from inside to outside. They can attempt to push and pull each other off-balance. One partner can move his or her arm out of the way to allow the other to thrust a hand forward to experience the sensation of occupying emptiness.

- *Boang Sao-Lop Sao*: This exercise, taken from Wing Chun, also has each partner keeping one arm in contact with a partner's opposing arm. While the first partner is grabbing the second partner's arm, lop sao, and throwing a backfist or straight punch, the second partner is using a boang sao, or deflecting block, against it. The second partner then grabs the first partner's arms and throws a backfist or straight punch, which the first partner deflects with a boang sao. The partners take turns in this manner. There are also ways for one partner to initiate a switch so that they flow smoothly into using the other arm. The drill helps you practice using the lop sao to grab and the boang sao to defend.

- Harmonious Spring: This drill was taken from the praying mantis system. There are one-arm and two-arm versions of the drill that are used. In the one-arm version, you can employ what is known as bridging energy against your partner's strike. Alternately, you can practice using what is known as dissolving energy against the strike. In the two-arm version, you use springing energy to prevent your partner from striking you with both hands.

- Swing Gate: In this drill, as you hold an arm out in punching position, your partner applies an inward forehand block against either the outside or inside of that arm. As your arm is being blocked, you must respond with a particular trap and punch. If your partner applies a block to the outside of your arm, you must utilize what is known as an elbow hinge to bring your arm back. As your rear hand grabs the blocking arm, you then snap your punching arm forward as if to strike. Alternately, if your partner applies a block to the inside of your punching arm, then you utilize the ball and socket joint of your arm to let the block go through. You then trap the arm with your rear hand and fire a backfist with your lead arm.

Simple Traps

When a Jeet Kune Do fighter employs one trap to facilitate one strike, that is known as a simple trap. You begin training in HIA by learning various simple traps. Initially, you train on these traps from a reference point, that is, from a touching position in which you assume that your partner has already blocked your punch. This is to help you learn the proper structure, mechanics, and distance required for the trap. As you become more proficient, you open up the distance and fire a punch from medium range, run into a barrier, then trap

Trapping as Disease

While trapping is fascinating and enjoyable to study, students of Jeet Kune Do must be careful not to get carried away with it. It needs to be placed in its proper context in the overall scheme of the art. Otherwise, rather than being a cure, it becomes a disease.

from there. Later, you can open up the distance even more and begin with a kicking-to-punching combination to move you into range to trap. In that way, you are able to employ trapping when moving from other distances and other ways of attack.

The following are simple traps you will learn when training in HIA.

- Pak Sao: This is known as slapping hand. The basic idea is that, when your partner's arm blocks the forward movement of your punch, your rear hand removes the barrier by slapping the arm forward and out of the way. This enables your punch to continue on its path toward the target.

Typically, when you first learn pak sao, you start at a high reference point. This means that you and your partner have your front hands up, touching on the outside just below the wrists. This is to simulate the situation in which one partner's lead punch to the face is blocked by the other partner's front arm.

As you touch, your front arm should apply forward pressure against your partner's front arm, which should provide some resistance. With your rear guard up, you shoot your rear hand forward at your partner's forearm and slap it away. You must ensure that you slap the arm forward toward your partner's centerline. You should brace the arm against your partner's body to keep it trapped so that your partner cannot use that arm. If you incorrectly slap it downward, your opponent can disengage it and counter with a hooking strike.

The moment that you immobilize your partner's arm, your lead punch should fire (see Figure 17-1). These movements should be coordinated with push shuffle advance footwork, because you will need to close on your opponent in order to land your punch. As you move in, you must ensure that you maintain the structural integrity of the lower-body bai-jong position. You should not end up with both feet closer together than before, but keep them at the same distance. You should not lean forward into your punch, which will disrupt your balance and possibly allow your partner to pull you.

Figure 17-1: Pak sao and lead punch

Figure 17-2: Lop sao and rear punch

- Pak sao can also be trained from a low reference point, in which both you and your partner are touching with your hands facing downward. This simulates your position if you tried a punch to the midsection, but your opponent's front arm did a downward block of that punch. In this scenario you step forward with push shuffle and use your rear hand to trap your partner's arm. As you do so, your lead hand swings back and upward into a backfist to your opponent's face (see Figure 17-2).

- Lop Sao: This is known as grabbing hand. The idea is that you immobilize your opponent's arm by grabbing it near the wrist and pulling the arm toward you. As you do so, your other arm can land a punch. Simultaneously yanking your opponent in your direction while firing a punch toward the face increases the power of your strike.

  Usually you learn this trap by starting at the high reference point with your partner, who provides either stiff resistance or forward-moving energy. When you feel this energy, you turn your hand to grab your partner's wrist. You should rotate your waist as you pull your partner's arm, yanking it toward you. At the same time you fire a rear straight punch to the face, extending your rear shoulder so that you can reach your partner with the punch.

- Jao Sao: This is known as running hand. Your front hand disengages from an attached position and moves to another position. For example, you can travel from a high line to a low line, from an outside line to an inside line, or an inside line to an outside line.

You train in a basic jao sao by starting at a high reference point with your partner. You disengage your front hand by moving it underneath your partner's front hand. You then shoot your front hand forward toward your partner's head. As you do so, your rear hand should move up to pick up your partner's front hand, to keep it from striking you. Then, if your partner's rear arm blocks your front hand, you can disengage your front hand and execute a front groin smash with your front palm.

- Jut Sao: Known as jerking hand, this is a quick, abrupt motion used to move one or both of your opponent's arms out of the way of your strike. You can use it to clear the arms so that you can strike at an open target area, or you can jerk your opponent's body downward as you execute a head butt or upward knee strike.

Figure 17-3: Jut sao and rear punch

You can jut sao either one arm or both arms. There are different types of exercises that beginning students can practice to learn the jut sao. For a single-arm jut sao, you can start with your lead hand touching the outside of your partner's front arm as you stand in unmatched lead. You can employ the jerking motion to clear the lead arm and return with a lead straight punch. Or from a matched lead, you can jerk down the rear arm while firing a rear straight punch at the same time (see Figure 17-3).

For a double-arm jut sao, you start with both of your hands in contact with the outside of your partner's arms. You can jerk down on both arms at the same time, clearing the line for different follow-ups. For example, you can execute a head butt as you jerk your partner's arms. Another option is to jerk the arms and then push the shoulders with the palms of both hands. You may choose to jerk the arms down as you fire a front knee strike to the chest. An additional option is to trap both arms with one of your arms and fire a punch with the other arm.

- *Huen Sao*: This is also known as circling hand. It is a disengagement of your hand from the outside of your opponent's arm to the inside, or vice versa, by circling your arm either over or under your opponent's arm. The purpose is to move your hand into a position from which you can execute a desired strike.

You can train for this by having your front hand on the outside of your partner's rear arm and your rear hand on the outside of your partner's front arm. You can circle your front hand over your partner's rear arm and clear it, so your front hand ends up on the inside position. From there your rear arm can trap both your partner's arms as your front hand fires a lead punch at your opponent.

In a variation of this drill, you distract your partner as you execute your huen sao. You do this by firing a rear punch at your opponent while you move your front hand to clear your partner's rear arm (see Figure 17-3). You then continue as before.

Figure 17-4: Huen sao and rear punch

Compound Traps

When a Jeet Kune Do fighter uses two or more traps in sequence, that is known as compound trapping. There are many compound traps that Jeet Kune Do students can study and execute. These drills help students learn to flow from one trap to another according to an opponent's responses. The basic idea is that, after you apply an initial trap and strike, if your partner obstructs the strike with another parry or block, you must trap that secondary barrier in order to strike.

Students will normally not learn compound trapping until they have become proficient in simple traps. The following are a few examples of compound traps taught in Jeet Kune Do.

- Pak Sao to Pak Sao: You initially trap your partner's lead arm and resume your punch. Your partner's rear arm then executes an inside block against the outside of your punching arm. The block stops at the centerline in this case. To clear the rear arm, your rear palm must slap it away. Then you can resume your punch.
- Pak Sao to Lin Lop Sao: This time, after you pak sao your partner's lead arm and you punch, your partner's rear arm does a wide inside block against your punching arm. In this case the block crosses the centerline. Your front arm should do an elbow hinge back as your rear hand grabs the blocking arm. As you lop sao that arm, you whip your front hand into a backfist.
- Lop Sao to Lop Sao: As you lop sao your partner's front arm and fire your rear punch, your partner's rear arm blocks the punch. Your rear hand then grabs the wrist of your partner's rear arm and yanks it forward as your front hand releases your partner's front arm and fires a lead punch.
- Jao Sao to Jut Sao: As your front hand disengages from your partner's front arm and tries a strike to the head, your partner's rear arm blocks it. From there you use your hands to jerk down on both of your partner's arms to clear them.

Lee on Training from the Reference Point

" If any student does his pak sao [or any technique for that matter] with wasted motion, back to the touching hand position he goes to minimize his unnecessary motions. So you see that in order to progress to apply pak sao from a distance, this touching hand position has to be mastered." (Lee 1997, p. 310)

There are many more compound trap sequences that you can learn, but these give you a flavor of how one trap can flow into another trap, depending upon how your opponent responds. In a real fighting situation, often one or, at most, two traps will be sufficient to allow you to strike your opponent.

In most circumstances you are not looking to trap, but to hit. HIA comes into play when you run into an obstruction as you try to hit your opponent. Therefore, as you train in HIA, remember that it is not an end in itself, but rather a means to an end. It is another useful way of attack that you can apply when your opponent gives you the appropriate opening.

Other Immobilization Attacks

We normally think of trapping as immobilizing the hands and arms. However, Jeet Kune Do also includes immobilization of other parts of the body. One of these is leg immobilization, which traps the opponent's legs to prevent kicking and moving. Also, hair immobilization involves grabbing the opponent's hair to control his head.

part 5
tactical considerations

S O FAR, we have considered the various tools of Jeet Kune Do strictly from an offensive viewpoint. However, because real combat does not permit a person to do nothing but attack, we must consider what a student can do when he or she is on the receiving end of an attack. So the next two chapters will deal with the different ways of defending yourself against an attack, as well as ways to counterattack against an aggressor.

Following those chapters, we will look at the important elements of distance, timing, and rhythm. These qualities help answer the questions of where and when to employ the various tools within a fighting context. Applying and integrating the many elements of Jeet Kune Do in more realistic circumstances require you to engage in sparring. In particular, we will look at how sparring, particularly specific sparring drills, can help you to use what you have learned against someone who is resisting and fighting back.

I
N SPORTS a team with a great offense that can score points can still lose if it cannot prevent the opposing team from scoring more points. So, in addition to having a solid offensive plan, a balanced team must have effective defensive skills. The same is true in combat. Even if you have a strong ability to attack, there will come a time when you must defend yourself against an opponent's attacks or counterattacks. If you have not developed your defensive capability, you may be defeated or hurt, no matter how good your offensive skills may be.

Thus, while Jeet Kune Do emphasizes attacks and counterattacks against an opponent, the development of defensive skills is also important. Fortunately, Bruce Lee did not consider such skills as merely an incidental part of his overall art. Rather, it is an important and integral aspect of the total package. There is an entire group of defensive methods that Lee incorporated into Jeet Kune Do.

These defensive methods can be broken down into several general categories. One is the use of footwork to avoid being hit. A second one is the employment of parrying to deflect an attack. A third one utilizes evasive body movements to steer clear of a strike. We will examine each of these below.

Most focus mitt drills used in the beginning of Jeet Kune Do training are geared toward developing offensive tools. Nevertheless, even at that stage, you can practice defenses by having your partner throw both punches with the gloves and light kicks.

Footwork

In Jeet Kune Do footwork plays an important role—not only in moving you into range where you can score, but also in moving you out of the path of your opponent's attack or counterattack. With footwork you can open up the distance so that your opponent's strike falls short of hitting you. You can also use footwork to move off-angle against your opponent's attack, which leaves you in position to counterattack.

If you want to open up the distance so that an attack cannot reach the target, you can use different types of footwork to move outside of your opponent's range. For example, if your opponent throws a lead punch at your head, you can use a push shuffle retreat to quickly move your body back. If your opponent throws a lead side kick at you, you need to move farther back, so you would use a slide step retreat, which covers more ground, to account for the longer reach of your opponent's lead leg. Still, another type of footwork you can use is a step-through retreat, in which you step back with your front leg and end up in a different lead.

The use of footwork to avoid your opponent's strikes has the added benefit of frustrating your opponent psychologically. When an attacker sees that you can consistently evade the strikes aimed at you, he or she can become upset, and an emotionally worked up opponent will not think clearly. It is generally easier to attack someone who is distracted by feelings of frustration.

Parrying

In parrying you use your hand to deflect an attack off of its path. You can utilize either your front or rear hand to parry your opponent's strike. A parry is different from a block in that a block is usually a hard movement that uses force against force. A parry, on the other hand, is a lighter movement that moves an attack off-line and does not require a large expenditure of energy.

Ideally, when you parry your opponent's strike, you want to wait until the very last moment, when it is about to hit, before you deflect it. Timing is a crucial element in a successful parry. If you see a strike coming and try to parry too early, you will miss the striking limb altogether and the strike will hit you. Also, when you parry too early, your opponent can switch the direction of the attack and score along a different line. However, if you start your parry too late, you will not deflect the strike in time to avoid being hit.

Distance is another important element for successful parrying. In some cases you may want to retreat as you parry, in order to open the distance. This can provide added safety, especially if your opponent has a long reach. In other cases you may want to advance in order to close the distance as you parry, in order to counterattack. You have to gauge the correct moment in which to parry your opponent's attack, so as not to run into his attack.

A parry can move laterally (for example, from left to right or vice-versa) against a punch. It can also be used in a semicircular fashion, in which you move your hand from high to low or low to high to deflect the strike. Sometimes you can use the parry with a slight upper-body lean or a short sidestep to give you more distance to avoid the strike.

In executing the parry you must take care to use small movements. However, if your parry is too small, it will not deflect the opponent's strike sufficiently, so you can still be hit. If you over-parry, that is, use too large a movement, then when you deflect the strike, your opponent can use your energy to change the line of attack and score. In some cases your over-parry can knock your opponent's striking limb into your own limb, which you might be using to counterattack.

Against an experienced fighter, Lee advises varying your parries and the types of defenses that you use. This will keep your opponent guessing and hesitating, which will affect the strength of his or her confidence and penetration.

An effective way to use a parry is to combine it with a counterstrike that occurs at the same time. This is known as a simultaneous parry and strike, which is more efficient than parrying first and then striking afterward. In Jeet Kune Do we use Four Corners training to develop the skill of concurrent hitting and parrying. Lee incorporated this concept from Wing Chun, which views the upper body as being divided into four sectors, or gates. Each of these gates is an area in which an opponent can strike. You can defend each of these gates with a different rear-hand parry. The upper gates are defended with high, upward parries, while the lower gates are defended by low, downward parries. As your opponent launches a punch into these different gates, you employ the appropriate parry to deflect the punch. At the same time you counterattack with your own lead punch.

Evasion

There are numerous types of movements, drawn largely from Western boxing, that you can use to avoid an opponent's attack. The idea is to shift and angle your body to avoid your opponent's blows, while remaining at a distance to launch a counterattack. Thus, evasion differs from a footwork retreat, which enables you to open up the distance to avoid a strike, but prevents you from counterattacking unless you move back into the proper range. The following are the basic evasions used in Jeet Kune Do.

- Ducking: This is a simple maneuver that can be used when an opponent swings or hooks a punch at your head. You move underneath the arc of the punch by bending your knees and dropping your body down to avoid being hit. Although you can lean your upper body forward slightly for added safety, you should avoid leaning too far because you will be off-balance.

  As you drop down, you should keep your head up and your hands high to protect your head. Your eyes should be focused in front toward your opponent (see Figure 18-1). This is important because you need to guard against the possibility that your opponent will strike you with a knee as you duck. You also have to be aware that your opponent might slam a fist, elbow, or forearm into your neck as you duck. Therefore, after you duck down and your opponent's arm has passed, quickly spring up from your feet and continue from there.

Figure 18-1: Duck against hook punch

- Slipping: This maneuver is used primarily against straight punches fired at your head. It involves a slight angulation of your upper body to either side of the punch, as it extends, so that the punch misses. For safety reasons it is preferable to slip to the outside, rather than to the inside, of the punch. When you slip to the outside, you basically isolate your opponent so that his or her other hand will be difficult to use against you. You only have to deal with the punching hand. However, when you slip to the inside, you have to concern yourself not only with the punching hand, but also with the other hand. You are putting yourself in a position where you can be hit by the other hand when you slip inside.

To slip to the outside against an opponent's right lead punch, you rotate at the waist and turn your right shoulder slightly to the left, forward, and down. In this way the punch travels just over your right shoulder and goes past your right ear. To slip to the inside against the same punch, you rotate at the waist and turn your left shoulder slightly to the right, forward, and down. In this way the punch travels just over your left shoulder and goes past your left ear.

To successfully slip a punch, you must have both good timing and proper distance. Good timing means that you wait until the very last moment before you slip the punch, so that your opponent is committed to the action and cannot stop in midstream. If you slip too early, your opponent can redirect the punch along a different path to your new position. Also, he or she can halt and wait until you return to your upright position and resume the strike. Either way, you will be hit. If you slip too late, you will not move your head away in time before the punch arrives, and you will be hit. So, you must gauge the right moment in which to initiate your slip.

Proper distance means that you must judge the right distance at which to slip the punch so that the punch goes over your shoulder and you are in range to counterattack. If you are too far away when you slip the punch, you have not accomplished anything, because the punch would have fallen short of you anyway. Also, you will likely be out of range to counterattack. If you are too close when you try to slip, you may misjudge the amount of time it will take for the punch to reach you. You may slip too late and be hit by the punch.

A slip normally does not engage your hands, so you are free to use either hand to strike your opponent. However, in some instances, you may wish to combine your slip with a front- or rear-hand parry, for added safety. Even if you parry the punch while you slip, your other hand will still be free to counterattack. Another way to increase your safety is to combine a small sidestep with the slip. This opens up the distance a little bit farther from the punch but keeps you in range to counterstrike.

One of the advantages of slipping a punch is that you can counter-attack, either immediately after the slip or at the same time that you slip. For instance, if you slip to the outside against your opponent's lead punch, your lead hand can fire a simultaneous low punch to the mid-section (see Figure 18-2).

If you slip the punch to the inside, your rear hand can fire a simultaneous rear cross to your opponent's midsection. Alternately, immediately after slipping the punch to the inside, you can follow with a lead hand shovel hook to the kidney or solar plexus.

Figure 18-2: Slip your opponent's punch and fire low punch

- Bob and Weave: In this maneuver you bend your knees and drop your body forward at the waist, to move underneath your opponent's swing or hooking punch to your head. This is known as the bob. As in the duck, as you bend your knees and drop down, keep your head up and your hands high. Keep your eyes focused in front toward your opponent. You need to be aware of the possibility that your opponent may try to throw a knee strike or a downward strike with a fist, elbow, or forearm while you are bobbing.

As your opponent's arm goes past your head, you swing your body to the outside of the punch, and rise back up behind the arc of the punch. This movement is known as the weave. It puts you in a spot to the outside of your opponent's attacking arm, where you can counter with your own strikes, but you must keep your guard up against any strikes from your opponent's other hand.

If your opponent swings from your left to your right, you bob and weave to your left so that you end up outside the punch as it passes. Then you can strike your opponent along the right side. If your opponent swings from your right to your left, you bob and weave to your right, ending up outside the punch as it passes. This time, you can strike your opponent along the left side. You can combine the weave with a small sidestep, both to move you more rapidly outside the punch and to put you in a better position to counterstrike.

- Snap-Away: Another maneuver that is useful against straight punches is the snap-away. As the punch is thrown at your head, you quickly move your head and upper torso back to avoid being hit. You accomplish this by combining the snap-away with a heel-toe sway, in which you drop your rear heel down and raise your front heel (see Figure 18-3). As the punching arm retracts, you can rapidly move your head and torso back into their initial positions.

Figure18-3: Snap-away with heel-toe sway against lead punch

You can snap forward and punch with your lead hand when your opponent retracts his or her arm. This requires good timing and proper distance to accomplish. For added safety, you should have your rear hand high to parry the punch if it comes too close to your face. For even more security you can combine the snap-away with a slight footwork retreat, which can open up the distance, especially if your opponent uses a deeper punch such as a rear cross.

Blocking or Covering

The final type of defensive maneuver used in Jeet Kune Do is blocking, or covering. This involves placing something in the path of the strike, such as an arm or a leg. In blocking or covering your limb basically absorbs the force of the hit. You should generally use this type of defense only when you are unable to employ one of the others. Even if you manage to block or cover against a hit, it can still hurt you and disrupt your balance. You will still absorb the punishment of the blow, but on your limb rather than your head or other part of your body.

As an example, when your opponent throws a lead hook punch at your head, you can raise your elbow and press your forearm against your head to protect it against the blow. You will still feel the blow, but your arm will absorb most of the force. You can combine this with a small step away from the punch to reduce the impact of the blow.

Similarly, if your opponent throws a lead hook kick to your ribs, you can drop your elbow down to protect your body against the kick. Your arm will receive the brunt of the kick and absorb most of the force. Again, you can combine this with a small step away from the kick (see Figure 18-4).

Figure 18-4: Cover against lead hook kick

Against a midlevel kick you can lift your leg so that the kick lands on your lower leg. This will protect your body as your lower leg receives the brunt of the kick. You want to avoid having the kick land directly upon your shin, however, because the impact of the kick upon the nerves there will be quite painful.

Despite all your training, there will be times when your defenses will fail you and you will be hit. Part of your education in fighting is to learn to absorb hits and endure pain. Learning from these mistakes can spur your growth and improve your fighting skills.

Although Jeet Kune Do stresses excellent attack skills, the student of Lee's art must also develop solid defensive capabilities as well. Just as specific ways of attack are more successful against certain types of fighters than against others, you must also vary your defenses according to the type of opponent you face. This requires you to develop a wide range of defensive skills and strategies from which to draw. The better you can adapt to different opponents, the more likely you will be to mount an effective defense against them.

The best way to become adept at defending yourself is to spar regularly. Nothing develops your defensive capabilities quite as rapidly as having someone throw punches and kicks at you. You learn very quickly to keep your hands up and your feet very mobile. Also, you heighten your awareness of your opponent's intentions.

A COUNTERATTACK is a type of advanced attack that you employ as your opponent is in the midst of attacking you. Whenever an offensive move is made against you, your opponent necessarily, if only momentarily, exposes some target area that you can strike. Your opponent is more vulnerable at that time because an attacker's attention must be concentrated more on offensive than defensive actions. Therefore, that moment represents a prime opportunity for you to land a strike upon your opponent.

Counterattacking often combines defensive moves with offensive moves. The defensive moves can include parrying, slipping, bobbing and weaving, and ducking. The offensive moves can involve kicks, punches, traps, and grappling. The basic idea is that you use your defensive skills to avoid being hit by your opponent. At the same time you employ your offensive tools to attack your opponent at the vulnerable spot. Before you can successfully utilize counterattacks, you must develop both your offensive skills and your defensive skills.

> "Though your style should be a combination of offense and defense, I often stress that offense should be the more emphasized. This does not mean that we should neglect defense; actually, as the reader will later realize, into every Jeet Kune Do offense, defense is also welded in to form what I term 'defensive offense.'" (Lee 1997, p. 64)

There are two basic types of counterattacks: offensive counterattacks and defensive-offensive counterattacks. We will examine each of these below.

Offensive Counterattacks

This type of counterattack is an offensive movement that simultaneously defends against your opponent's attack and attacks your opponent in the midst of his attack. Offensive counterattacks consist primarily of the stop-hit and the stop-kick. The stop-hit is a lead straight punch that you direct at your opponent's face as he or she is trying to punch you or kick you. The stop-hit defends against your opponent's attack by disrupting the forward movement of the attack. At the same time it attacks your opponent by striking a vulnerable target area. The stop-hit is a perfect example of the principle of intercepting your opponent's attack. The following are some examples of the stop-hit applied against specific situations.

> **B**ruce Lee considered the offensive type of counterattack, namely, the stop-hit, or stop-kick, to be the highest essence of his evolved approach to fighting. Thus, he named his art "Jeet Kune Do," translated "the way of the intercepting fist," to reflect this. However, he later regretted giving it a name, because he found even this to be too limiting.

- Stop-Hit against Forward Advance: As your opponent begins to step toward you preparing to punch or kick you, you fire a lead straight punch to the face. This effectively halts the forward movement and disrupts your opponent's intentions.
- Stop-Hit against Lead Punch: As your opponent starts to fire a lead punch toward you, you intercept with a lead straight punch to the face. This disrupts your opponent's attack and prevents the punch from striking you.
- Stop-Hit against Rear Cross: This time, as your opponent starts to throw a rear cross, you intercept with a lead straight punch to the face. Your opponent is unable to successfully complete the rear cross because you have halted his or her momentum.
- Stop-Hit against Wide Looping Hook Punch: In this situation as your opponent takes a swing with a wide looping punch, you intercept with a lead straight punch to the face. Your punch hits within the circumference of the swing and should, therefore, reach your opponent first. For safety, you can put up your rear hand to parry your opponent's arm.
- Stop-Hit between Motions: You can also execute a stop-hit in-between your opponent's motions. For example, suppose your opponent throws a

lead punch and follows with a lead hook punch. You can parry or evade the lead punch. Then, as your opponent starts to throw the lead hook punch, you intercept with a lead straight punch to the face.

- Stop-Hit at Opponent's Feint: If your opponent executes a feint, you can stop-hit it with a lead straight punch to the face as he or she executes the feint. This shuts down any follow-up attack that your opponent intended. The stop-kick operates in a similar way to the stop-hit. You can execute a side kick to your opponent's body to halt your opponent in the midst of an attack. The following are examples of the stop-kick.
- Stop-Kick against Forward Advance: As your opponent starts to step toward you preparing to kick or punch you, you fire a lead side kick to the front shin. This effectively halts the forward momentum and disrupts your opponent's intentions.
- Stop-Kick against Straight Punch: As your opponent starts to launch a lead straight punch to your face, you fire a lead side kick to the midsection (see Figure 19-1). This disrupts your opponent's attack and halts the forward movement. The stop-kick

Figure 19-1: Stop-kick against straight punch

can be executed against the lead punch whether your opponent is in matched lead or unmatched lead.

- Stop-Kick against Rear Cross: This time, as your opponent fires the rear cross, you intercept with a lead side kick to the front shin or to his or her midsection. Be sure that, as you execute the kick, you lean back away from the rear cross. Your kick disrupts your opponent's punch. In both the stop-hit and the stop-kick, there are certain elements that must work together in order for the conterattack to be effective. These are as follows.
- Timing: This is a critical element, without which you cannot stop-hit or stop-kick successfully. You must launch your punch or kick at the right moment, when your opponent is advancing toward you and is either

preparing to attack or starting to attack. If you launch your counterattack too early, your opponent may see it and pause until he or she can resume the attack. In that case your stop-hit or stop-kick will not strike your opponent or disrupt the attack. If you launch your counterattack too late, your punch or kick might be jammed and be ineffectual in stopping your opponent, who will continue to close and strike you.

- Distance: This is another element that is important. When you fire your stop-hit or stop-kick, you must be at a distance where it can actually reach your intended target area, in order to halt your opponent or disrupt the attack. If you are too far from your opponent when you launch your counterattack, it will fall short of the target and fail to stop the attack. However, if you are too close to your opponent when you launch the counterattack, your punch or kick can be jammed and lack the power needed to stop your opponent. Make sure that you use the proper body mechanics behind your punch or kick to help ensure that it has adequate reach.

- Speed: In order for your stop-hit or stop-kick to reach your opponent in time to halt the attack, you must execute your punch or kick with sufficient speed. You should train to minimize the amount of time required for you to react to your opponent's attack and fully extend your punch or kick. If your speed is too slow, then your stop-hit or stop-kick will not strike before your opponent can close in and attack you.

- Power: You must have sufficient power behind your stop-hit or stop-kick so that your opponent will actually be stopped in mid-attack. If your punch or your kick is weak, your opponent will simply move through it and advance toward you. You can develop power by applying speed and proper body mechanics when you throw your punch or kick.

Defensive-Offensive Counterattacks

The other category of counterattacks is known as defensive-offensive. These counterattacks differ from the strictly offensive counterattacks in that they have a "defensive" element to them. There are four specific types of defensive-offensive counterattacks: (1) evade and counter, (2) parry and counter, (3) jam and counter, and (4) time-hit. We will examine each of these below.

Evade and Counter

This specific type of counterattack is a two-step process. First, you defend against an opponent's attack by taking evasive action, such as footwork or body movement and angulation, so that the attack misses. You then follow with your own attack, normally a punch or a kick. The following are examples of this type of counterattack.

- Slip Rear Cross to Rear Shovel Hook: Your opponent faces you in a mismatched lead. As your opponent throws a rear cross, you slip to the outside so that the punch misses and goes over your right shoulder. This puts you off to your opponent's right side. From there, you execute a rear shovel hook to your opponent's kidney area.
- Split Entry against Lead Punch to Lead Shovel Hook: Your opponent faces you in an unmatched lead. As he or she throws a lead punch at your face, you step to the right so that the punch misses and goes over your left shoulder. At the same time, you throw a rear cross at your opponent's face. You follow with a lead shovel hook to your opponent's kidney area.
- Retreat against Lead Side Kick to Lead Side Kick: Your opponent throws a lead side kick at you, which you evade by stepping back so that it falls short and misses you. As your opponent is in the midst of recovering from the side kick, you follow with a lead side kick to the midsection.

Parry and Counter

In this type of counterattack, you defend against your opponent's attack by parrying it with one hand. You attack your opponent with your other hand.

For example, suppose that your opponent throws a lead hook punch at your head. You can hold up your rear hand to deflect the punch as your front hand fires a lead straight punch at your opponent's face. There are three possible timings that can occur. First, you can deflect the hook punch

> Daniel Lee, a student from the Los Angeles Chinatown school, has stated that the simultaneous parry and hit was an improvement over the block and go systems to which most of the students were accustomed.

first and then throw the lead straight punch immediately afterwards. Second, you can deflect the hook punch and throw the lead straight punch at the same time. Third, you can hit with the lead straight punch and follow with a deflection of the hook punch.

Jam and Counter

This type of counterattack requires you to crash into your opponent's attacking line to prevent him or her from executing an attack. This puts you into close range, where you can follow with your own attack, such as a grappling technique. For instance, as your opponent's front leg rises in preparation to kick, you suddenly and swiftly move in to smother the kick by lifting your own front leg and placing it against your opponent's leg. As you do so, you must keep your hands up to protect your high line from any punches. As you step down, you can quickly maneuver to your opponent's back and execute a rear neck stranglehold. You can also use your front arm to execute a lead forearm smash against the face or chest and bring your opponent down.

Time-Hit

The final type of defensive-offensive counterattack is called the time-hit. As the name suggests, you execute your counterattack at the exact moment when your opponent attacks you. The defensive aspect comes into play because you prevent the attack from landing by deflecting your opponent's limb. The same technique that you use to deflect the attack simultaneously lands your own attack upon your opponent. You accomplish this by employing a sliding leverage hit, which cuts across your opponent's attacking tool to keep it from hitting you, while at the same time allowing you to strike your opponent.

Figure 19-2: Sliding leverage finger jab against lead punch

For instance, assume that your opponent faces you in unmatched lead. As he or she throws a lead punch at your face, you sidestep slightly to your right and fire a lead finger jab to the face. Your lead arm cuts across your opponent's lead arm, deflecting the punch away from you. As your lead arm slides over your opponent's lead arm, your front fingers strike your opponent's eyes (see Figure 19-2).

Suppose this time that your opponent, again in unmatched lead, throws a rear cross at your face. You step off to your left and fire a rear straight punch to the face. Your rear arm cuts across your opponent's rear arm, deflecting the rear cross away from you. As your rear arm slides over your opponent's rear arm, your rear fist strikes your opponent's face.

Counterattack Drills

There are numerous drills that students of Jeet Kune Do can practice with a partner to strengthen skills in the various ways of counterattacking. These drills are useful for developing a good sense of timing and distance, as well as developing proper body mechanics and an ability to flow from defense to offense. They are practical in that they refine your counterattack ability against some of the more common types of attacks, namely, the jab to cross (one-two), jab to hook (one-three), lead side kick, and hook kicks. The following are examples of some of these drills.

Drills against Jab to Cross

These drills are responses against an opponent who throws a lead jab to your face and follows with a rear cross.

- Catch Jab, Slip Cross with Low Rear Cross: In this drill you first catch, or parry, your opponent's front-hand jab with your rear hand. Then, as the rear cross is fired, you slip the punch to the outside so that it misses and goes over your left shoulder. As you slip the punch, you throw your own rear cross to your opponent's midsection.
- Catch Jab, Slip Cross with High Rear Cross: In this situation you first catch, or parry, your opponent's front-hand jab with your rear hand. Then, as your opponent fires the rear cross, you slip the punch to the outside so that it misses and goes over your left shoulder. As you slip the punch, you throw your own rear cross to your opponent's face.
- Catch Jab, Lead Hook Punch to Head: You catch, or parry, your opponent's front-hand jab with your rear hand. As the rear cross is fired, you sidestep to the outside of the punch and throw a lead hook punch to your opponent's head. The hook punch should go over the rear arm and strike

Figure 19-3: Lead uppercut against rear cross

the head. Timing is important here because you want your lead hook punch to land just as your opponent's rear arm is reaching maximum extension.

- Catch Jab, Lead Uppercut: When your opponent throws the front jab, your rear hand catches or parries it. Then, when your opponent fires the rear cross, you sidestep to the outside and execute a lead uppercut to the chin. Your lead uppercut should go underneath your opponent's rear arm and up into the chin (see Figure 19-3). You should time the uppercut to strike the chin just as your opponent's rear arm reaches maximum extension.

- Catch Jab, Sliding Leverage Punch: You catch or parry your opponent's front hand jab with your rear hand. When your opponent throws the rear cross, you step off to the outside of it and execute a front-hand sliding leverage punch. The punch should slide across your opponent's rear arm and strike the face.

- Catch Jab, Boang Sao/Backfist: As your opponent fires the front-hand jab, you catch or parry it with your rear hand. When he or she throws the rear cross, your step off to the outside, raising your front arm into a boang sao to deflect the strike. Your rear hand then goes over your front arm to grab your opponent's rear arm. As you yank the arm, your front hand executes a backfist against your opponent's face.

Drills against Jab to Lead Hook Punch

These drills train various responses against an opponent who throws a lead jab and follows with a lead hook punch.

- Catch Jab, Duck, and Lead Punch: As your opponent throws the front hand jab, you catch or parry it with your rear hand. When the lead hook punch follows, you duck underneath it. As you are ducking, you fire a lead punch to your opponent's mid-section.

- Catch Jab, Cover, and Lead Punch: When your opponent throws the front hand jab, you catch or parry it with your rear hand. When the lead hook punch follows, your rear hand moves to the side of your head to cover against it. Your front hand fires a lead straight punch to your opponent's face.

- Catch Jab, Bob and Weave, and Cross, Hook, Cross: Your rear hand catches or parries your opponent's front hand jab. When your opponent throws the lead hook punch, you bob and weave under it. As you rise up behind the punch, you fire a rear cross, then a lead hook punch, then a rear cross, all to your opponent's head.

> If you stick to one type of counterattack, an experienced fighter may learn to anticipate your actions and counter your counterattack. Therefore, it is advisable to vary your counterattacks in order to make yourself more unpredictable.

Drills against Lead Side Kick

These drills train your various responses to an opponent who attacks you with a lead side kick.

- Retreat and Return Side Kick: As your opponent fires a lead side kick, you use slide step footwork to retreat so that the kick falls short. You can combine your movement with a downward parry of the kick with either your front or rear hand. As your opponent's front leg lands, but before he or she recovers completely, you launch your own side kick against the shin, knee, or midsection.

- Parry and Return Side Kick: As your opponent throws the lead side kick, you use either hand to do a downward parry of the kick, as you step off to the side. Then you return your own side kick to your opponent. If you use your front hand, you will parry the kick to your right as you step to your left, then follow with your side kick. If you use your rear hand, you will parry the kick to your left as you step to your right. Then follow with your side kick.

- Parry and Return Hook Kick: When your opponent throws the lead side kick, you can use either hand to parry it. You then follow with the appropriate hook kick to your opponent's support leg. If you use your front

Figure 19-4: Parry side kick and rear hook kick to support leg

hand, you do a downward parry to your right as you step left. You then counter with a lead hook kick to the support leg. If you use your rear hand, you do a downward parry to your left as you step right. You then follow with a rear hook kick to your opponent's support leg (see Figure 19-4).

Drills against Lead or Rear Hook Kick

The following drills are useful in developing your counterattacks against an opponent who throws either a lead or a rear hook kick.

- Retreat and Return Hook Kick/Side Kick: When your opponent fires a lead or rear hook kick, you use your footwork to retreat so that it falls short of hitting you. Then you advance to return your own lead hook kick or side kick against your opponent.
- Cover and Return Hook, Cross, Hook: If your opponent fires a lead hook kick to your ribs, your press your rear elbow against it to absorb the kick and protect the ribs. Then you step in and follow with a lead hook punch, rear cross, and lead hook punch to your opponent's head. If your opponent fires a rear hook kick instead, you press your front elbow against your ribs to protect them. Then you step in and follow with a rear cross, lead hook punch, and rear cross to the head.
- Parry and Return Hook Kick: When your opponent throws a lead hook kick, you can use your front hand to execute a downward parry to your right as you step to your left. Then follow with a lead hook kick to your opponent's support leg. If your opponent throws a rear hook kick, you can use your rear hand to execute a downward parry to your left as you step right. Then you follow with a rear hook kick to the support leg.

Counterattacking is a sophisticated way of attacking your opponent in the midst of an attack on you. It requires a strong sense of judgment, timing, speed, and accuracy to land your own strike at the vulnerable target area when your opponent is on the offensive. It blends the various offensive and defensive skills that you develop into an effective flow, so that both work together to allow you to accomplish your purpose.

Ted Wong, one of Lee's last major private students, used to spar quite a bit with Lee. Wong says that he became more of a counterfighter because it was too difficult to successfully attack Lee.

chapter 20
distance, timing, and rhythm

I T IS OFTEN SAID that success in any endeavor depends upon being in the right place at the right time. This is especially true in fighting. Even if you know thousands of techniques and can execute them flawlessly, they will do you no good if none of them actually reaches your opponent. On the other hand, you will have great difficulty defending yourself if you allow your opponent's strikes to consistently reach you. Your techniques will also be useless if you try to use them at a moment when your opponent can effectively defend against them. Therefore, in order to both attack and defend successfully, you must learn how to move into the proper distance relative to your opponent. You must also learn how to time your attacks so that they have the greatest probability of landing on your opponent. In addition, you need to learn to time your movements to prevent your opponent from striking you.

> Lee identified three things that are necessary for correct attacking: a keen sense of timing, good judgment of distance, and proper application of speed and rhythm. These all must be coordinated with your opponent's actions.

Learning how to execute the tools and weapons is important in the beginning, but the Jeet Kune Do student must move beyond the mere mechanical movements into application. This is where training in the use of distance, timing, and rhythm becomes very important. We will examine each of these qualities below.

Distance

In fighting, distance refers to the spatial relationship between a fighter and an opponent. When you want to successfully strike your opponent, you must either reduce the distance between you, so that you can land the strike, or you must wait for your opponent to reduce the distance, so that you can execute a counterstrike. When you want to avoid being hit, you have to increase your distance from your opponent. Thus, if you can control the distance between yourself and your opponent, in order to carry out these objectives, you will be the one who controls the fight.

The Three Ranges

In Jeet Kune Do distance is defined in terms of three ranges: (1) long range, (2) medium range, also known as intermediate range, and (3) close range. Long range refers to that distance at which neither you nor your opponent can touch each other. Both of you are just beyond reach of your longest weapons. In medium range you can reach your opponent with your longest kick and your longest punch. Finally, in close range you can trap your opponent's limbs and grapple with your opponent.

Certain techniques can only be executed when you are in the correct range. For example, if you want to attack with a side kick, you must enter into medium range in order to land it. In order to grapple, you must be in close range. An understanding of what you can and cannot do in each range is necessary so that you can use the appropriate techniques when you are in a given range.

The Fighting Measure

In order to determine how much distance you should have between yourself and your opponent, you can use a concept known in Jeet Kune Do as "the fighting measure." This refers to the distance, or length of space, that you intentionally maintain against your opponent in order to control the distance. The fighting measure depends on your own characteristics and those of your opponent. It can easily change according to who your opponent is.

Several factors will influence the fighting measure. First, you must consider the maximum reach of your longest weapon. For the high line your longest weapon is your lead finger jab. For the low line your longest weapon is your lead side kick. So, initially, you must think about how close you need to be in order to reach your opponent with these weapons.

Second, you have to consider the reach of your opponent's longest weapons. You must assess how far your opponent's longest hand strike can reach at full extension. Also, you need to evaluate how far your opponent's longest kick can reach at full extension. You want to make sure that you are just outside the range that these weapons could reach if your opponent were to attack with them. This will vary according to your opponent. For instance, if your opponent is much taller than you are, then his or her weapons will be able to reach a farther distance.

Third, you need to consider the target areas that you need to defend against your opponent's attacks. For instance, if your opponent is a puncher but not a kicker, then you only have to concern yourself with those targets that can be reached with the front hand. However, if your opponent is also a kicker, then you must also be aware of those targets that the lead foot can strike. You have to take into account the fact that your opponent's front kick can reach farther than the front hand.

Fourth, you must assess how quickly both you and your opponent can close the distance to strike each other. For example, if your opponent is relatively slow in advancing, you can afford to position yourself a little bit closer. Also, if your opponent tends to telegraph strikes, that gives you an early warning of his or her intentions, so you can stay closer. However, if an opponent is quick on his or her feet, then you will probably want to stay a little farther away for added safety.

Similarly, if you have quick footwork, you can close the distance from farther out and still strike your opponent. If you are slower, then you have to edge in closer in order to reach your opponent.

Breaking the Distance

After you have learned to control the distance, you can focus on breaking the distance. This basically means that you can adjust the distance to your advantage without letting your opponent become aware it. There are several methods that you can use to break the distance.

One way is to create a false sense of distance. You can deceive opponents into thinking that they are at a safe distance from your kicks or punches, when they are actually within range. This may cause an opponent to relax his or her guard, providing you with an opportunity to strike while your opponent is off guard.

For instance, you can fire a lead punch at your opponent that intentionally falls short of the target. You can do this by not rotating your hips or extending your shoulder fully when you reach apparent full extension. Your opponent will think that he or she is safely out of range of your strike, when you actually could have landed the strike. Then, at the right moment, you fire your lead punch with proper hip rotation and shoulder extension. The punch will strike your opponent, who will not be prepared to defend against it, because he or she thinks you are out of range.

Another way to break the distance is by adjusting your footwork to move you closer so that you can strike without your opponent expecting it. For example, you can use a type of footwork called "steal a step," which brings you nearer to your opponent than he or she believes. To execute this, you quietly and subtly bring your rear foot forward so it is just behind your front foot. To hide this movement, you can feint a hand strike such as a finger jab, which diverts your opponent's attention away from your feet and toward your hand. The position of your rear foot sets limits on how close you can be to your opponent. Therefore, when you move up your rear foot, you have, in effect, decreased your distance to your opponent.

According to Lee, a skilled fighter always keeps himself just out of reach of his opponent's attack. He always moves to make his opponent misjudge his distance. At the same time he remains sure of his own distance.

Because your opponent is unaware of the fact that you have advanced your rear foot, he or she still thinks that you are at the same distance as before. From this position you can execute a push shuffle to launch a front hand strike. Alternately, you can launch a front leg kick from your new position.

Another way to adjust your footwork is to use progressively shorter steps each time you retreat from your opponent. This can work well if your opponent advances toward you each time you retreat. If your opponent steps forward the same amount of distance each time you move back, and you shorten your back step each time, your opponent can unknowingly move into range for a counterattack. Once your opponent has moved within range, you can execute a lead straight punch or a lead shin kick.

A final way to break the distance is by employing broken rhythm. The idea is that you first establish a rhythm with your opponent, in which his or her movements are synchronized with yours. You can then break the rhythm by either suddenly speeding up or slowing down. For a moment your opponent is less guarded because his or her movement is slightly behind or slightly ahead of your movement. It is during this moment that you can execute and land a strike.

Using Distance in Attack

To properly use distance in attacking, you need to know how to close the distance to your opponent is so you can land your attack. This is also known in Jeet Kune Do as "bridging the gap" between you and your opponent. For instance, if you are in long range, where you cannot touch your opponent, you have to learn how to quickly move into medium range in order to land your kick or punch. If you are in intermediate range, you need to learn how to move into close range if you want to trap, grapple, or use other tools such as the knees and elbows.

One way to bridge the gap is to hide your forward movement by using a feint or false attack. For example, you can fire a fake finger jab in order to distract your opponent. While your opponent's focus is on responding to your hand strike, you can use your footwork to quickly advance into range for a front leg kick.

Another way to bridge the gap is to use your longest weapon to hit your opponent's nearest target. For instance, you can move in while firing a lead finger jab to the eyes or a lead side kick to the front shin or knee. The action of firing these lead weapons, in itself, helps to close the distance and puts you into position to follow up with another technique.

Using Distance in Defense

To properly use distance as a way to defend, you need to know how to adjust your distance so that your opponent is unable to hit you. There are basically two ways to do this. One way is to open, or increase, the distance between you and your opponent so that any punch or kick that is thrown at you will fall short. You accomplish this by employing evasive footwork. For instance, if your opponent launches a lead side kick, you can quickly step back with a slide step retreat to avoid being hit (see Figure 20-1).

Another way to keep from being hit is by closing the distance through jam-

Figure 20-1: Retreat to open distance against side kick

Figure 20-2: Close distance by jamming an attack

ming your opponent. In essence, as your opponent prepares to attack, you quickly move forward to smother the attack and prevent its launch. From there you can follow up with a counterattack, such as grappling. For instance, if your opponent is about to throw a lead kick, you rapidly step in with your knee raised and brace it against your opponent's leg to keep the kick from firing (see Figure 20-2). From there you can step down and implement a takedown or a choke, for example.

Timing

Another quality that is essential for effective fighting is timing. This refers to sensing the right moment at which to launch an attack or counterattack. You will not be successful in landing strikes against opponents who are well guarded and able to protect themselves. You want to be able to hit when the desired target area is unprotected. This can occur when your opponent is transitioning from one position to another, or makes an error, or is forced to leave the target undefended because of some action that you initiate. In any case, you want to be able to recognize, and take advantage of, the specific moment when your opponent is most vulnerable to your strikes, either in attack or counterattack.

To develop the ability to sense these opportune moments for your attack or counterattack, you must learn to carefully observe your opponents. As you train with different partners, especially in sparring, watch their movements. As they step from one position to another, do they tend to leave certain areas unguarded? Do they move their arms in certain patterns that expose specific parts of the body? When they throw punches or kicks, which regions open up for a possible counterattack? By studying each partner in this way, you raise your awareness of when exact targets become vulnerable. These represent key moments in which you can successfully land a strike.

Reaction Time and Movement Time

It is not enough, however, to learn merely how to recognize the right moment to strike. Even if you develop this sense to a high degree, you still must be able to execute your techniques so that you can land your strikes within that moment. There are two types of timing that you can strengthen to improve your ability to take advantage of these moments. One is reaction time and the other is movement time.

Reaction time has to do with how quickly you can recognize an event and begin to respond to it. When you see or hear something, it takes time for your brain to process it and send signals to your body to take the appropriate action. In the context of fighting, when you see an opening in your opponent's defense, your brain must tell your arm or your leg to execute an appropriate strike to the exposed area. By reducing the amount of time required for this process to occur, you can speed up your reaction time and reach the target area more quickly.

Movement time refers to how long it takes you to execute a technique from beginning to end, once you have recognized the moment. If you are relatively slow in performing the technique, you may find that the target area has closed before you reach it. So you want to minimize the amount of time required for your technique to be completed.

One of the best ways for you to improve both your reaction time and your movement time is to practice focus-mitt drills with a partner. Your partner employs the mitts like flash cards, showing the mitts only at certain moments. When a mitt is displayed, it represents a moment when a target area is exposed. As soon as you see the mitt flashed, you fire the appropriate technique to strike the mitt. To make the drills more challenging, your partner can flash the mitt for a brief moment, such as a fraction of a second, before returning it to a neutral position. Then you have to really speed up your strike in order to hit the mitt before your partner takes it away. By practicing these drills regularly and consistently over a period of time, you can shorten your reaction time and tighten your movement time.

Use of Timing in Attack/Counterattack

You can time your attack or counterattack to correspond to certain stages of your opponent's attack. Generally, you can break down your opponent's attack into three stages: (1) preparation, (2) development, and (3) completion. As the name suggests, attack upon preparation refers to the beginning of your opponent's attack, as he or she is getting ready to execute the technique (see Figure 20-3). Attack upon development characterizes your opponent's attack as it is on its way toward the target. Finally, attack upon completion relates to the moment when your opponent has finished the technique and starts to recover. At each of these stages, you can execute an appropriate attack or counterattack to an exposed target area.

For instance, as your opponent prepares to fire a lead punch, you can close the distance and trap his or her front arm to prevent the punch from executing. At the same time you can fire your own lead straight punch to the face.

Figure 20-3: Attack on preparation—lead straight punch as opponent starts to throw lead hook

Distance and timing do not exist apart from how you relate to your opponent. Therefore, sparring is an excellent way to develop your ability to use distance and timing in fighting. You need a partner who will move and respond so that you can learn how to judge distance and how to time your attacks.

To help you understand and utilize rhythm to your advantage in combat, you should study music. You will develop a better understanding of cadence, beats, and half-beats, all of which relate to fighting. In addition, you will gain a greater appreciation for music as an art form.

If your opponent manages to launch a lead punch toward your face, you can use your rear hand to parry the punch as your lead hand counters with a low punch to the midsection. Finally, if your opponent fires the punch, misses, and begins to retract the punch, you can fire a quick lead backfist to the face while he or she is recovering. All these represent counterattacks that you can execute at the different stages of a single technique, namely, your opponent's lead punch.

Rhythm

A final quality that should be cultivated is rhythm, the tempo at which you move in a fight. Many fighters have a tendency to establish a uniform rhythm when they fight. They move according to a certain tempo or cadence. If you remain in the same rhythm as your opponent, it may be difficult for you to land a strike, because your opponent's defensive movements can track your offensive movements.

Your objective is to control the rhythm, because the person who controls the rhythm controls the fight. In Jeet Kune Do you control the rhythm by using what is known as "broken rhythm." As your opponent maintains a steady tempo, you can change your rhythm by pausing or speeding up your movements. In this way your rhythm is no longer synchronized with your opponent's rhythm. This allows you to insert your strikes in-between his or her movements (see Figures 20-4 and 20-5).

Breaking the rhythm is accomplished in two ways. First, you can speed up your movement relative to that of your opponent, catching your opponent unawares. Second, you can slow down your movement and pause in-between your opponent's movements. This also can catch your opponent off guard. If each of your opponent's movements is considered one beat, then you seek to strike in-between the beats, or on the half-beat.

The cultivation of fighting skills requires not only solid execution of your techniques, but also an understanding of proper distance, timing, and rhythm.

These qualities enable you to apply the techniques at the right moment, when you are in a good position to attack or counterattack your opponent. By training specifically with these qualities in mind, you learn how to relate to your opponent in a way that gives you the upper hand in a fight.

Figure 20-4: Catch opponent's lead punch

Figure 20-5: Followed by lead punch on half-beat as opponent starts to throw hook punch

A useful drill to help you understand distance involves throwing a lead shin kick at your opponent. When your sparring partner thinks you are about to fire it, he or she must retreat. The first few times, you will probably find yourself falling short because you are aiming at where your opponent was. You must compensate by figuring out where he or she will end up, because that is where to fire your kick.

sparring

EARNING THE INDIVIDUAL COMPONENTS of Jeet Kune Do, such as footwork, upper- and lower-body tools, the five ways of attack, defenses, counterattacks, distance, timing, and rhythm, are essential to developing a strong foundation in the art. However, further development and growth can only come by integrating these elements into practical, real-time application.

This is where sparring comes into play. Sparring is the activity in which you practice utilizing the tools within the five ways of attack against an opponent. It allows you to exercise your defensive and counterattack skills as your opponent tries to attack you. In sparring you cultivate a strong sense of the essential qualities of fighting technique, such as timing, distance, and rhythm.

It is important for you to understand what it is like to try to hit someone who is doing everything possible to avoid being hit. You need to become aware that your opponent will not stand in front of you, waiting for you to land your strikes. Opponents will be moving around, ducking, slipping, and covering, frustrating you at every turn. An opponent will also be looking for opportunities to hit you, throwing punches and kicks when he or she sees an opening. Thus, it is vital for you to know what it is like to have someone trying to hit you, so that you can make your defensive moves really count.

Sparring makes your training come alive, with energy and timing coming to the forefront. It is the way you learn to cultivate a fighting mindset and a proper attitude. You learn how to manage your emotions and your adrenal response so that you can maintain your composure and keep yourself relaxed.

Sparring is like a laboratory where you take different elements and experiment to test your theories and hypotheses. In sparring you try out different approaches and test your skills to see if you can really apply what you have learned against a live, resisting opponent. It can be compared to a mirror that allows you to see your strengths and flaws as they really are, clearly and truthfully. If, up to this point, you have been misled or, worst yet, have deceived yourself about your abilities, sparring will reveal the truth.

In the beginning sparring can be a humbling, even humiliating, experience. However, this process is necessary to convince you that there are areas that need improvement. It will not simply be a matter of your instructor pointing out these areas, for you yourself will become aware of them. This will provide you with the motivation that you need to correct your mistakes and perfect your skills.

> **S**parring should be viewed as an opportunity for both partners to learn and grow. If one partner is having difficulty dealing with the other partner's attacks, the other partner should slow down the pace to allow him or her to work at a comfortable pace. It is not about ego.

Sparring Progression

In Jeet Kune Do sparring is not simply a matter of throwing two people together and letting them have at it. Such an approach would be highly counterproductive and increase the chances of injury and of overblown egos. What was supposed to be an opportunity for learning would quickly become a brawl with no focus and no refinement. Rather than cool calculation, strategy, and tactics, hot emotions would rule.

Instead, sparring in Jeet Kune Do is trained in a progressive manner. It is done slowly, isolating and developing the individual tools and qualities in order to cultivate them to a high degree. The progressive approach also trains the mind and the emotions in an incremental manner by focusing them on just one or two things at a time, rather than overwhelming them with multiple concerns.

Sparring Drills

To introduce students to sparring, Jeet Kune Do makes use of sparring drills. These drills emphasize the execution of one tool, or just a few tools, in a more realistic environment in which you try to hit a live, resisting, moving opponent who is also trying to hit you. In the beginning, you start with very simple drills in which you and your opponent concentrate on training just one tool—for example, a lead punch. As you become comfortable at that level, you move on to slightly more complicated drills involving a few more tools. When you become proficient at these drills, you graduate to more complex drills involving multiple tools and ranges of combat. These drills start to approach and resemble freestyle sparring, which is the ultimate goal of your training.

The following is a look at some progressive sparring drills, beginning with the most simple and leading to more sophisticated ones.

Figure 21-1: Lead hand vs. lead hand sparring—split entry lead punch against the lead punch

- Lead Hand vs. Lead Hand: In this drill both students are limited to attacking or counterattacking with the lead hand. This means that you can only use front hand techniques such as the lead jab, lead straight punch, lead hook punch, lead backfist, lead uppercut, and lead shovel hook (see Figure 21-1). This is an excellent drill for students who are just starting out in sparring. They can concentrate on employing just one tool for striking. At the same time they only have to be concerned with defending against one tool utilized by their partner.

- Lead Hand vs. Both Hands: This represents a slightly more advanced drill. This time, one student is allowed to strike with both hands, while the other is limited to attacking or counterattacking with just the lead hand. This means that one student can execute both lead hand strikes and rear hand strikes. While this student only has to be concerned with defending against front hand strikes, the other student has to be aware of both the front hand and the rear hand in order to defend against both.

- Lead Hand vs. Lead Foot: In this drill one student can only employ the front hand to strike. The other student can use only the front leg to kick.

In terms of defense, when you are the one who can kick, you only have to be concerned with attacks from the front hand. At the same time you can take advantage of the longer reach of the front leg, which gives you the edge in distance. Because of this, when you are in the other position, you have to keep a longer distance away from your partner, in order to avoid being kicked. You also have to learn how to close from this distance in order to punch.

Lee was an innovator in the use of equipment during sparring. He utilized headgear, gloves, chest guards, and shin/knee guards. This enabled him and his students to go all out with full contact.

- Lead Hand vs. Lead Hand and Lead Foot: The sophistication of the training is growing with this drill. This time, one student is limited to using the front hand to strike, while the other student can employ both the front hand and the front foot. In one role you have more striking tools that you can employ to hit at the high line, midline, and low line. In the other role you have to be aware of a strike coming from almost anywhere, and you must also maintain a distance to protect against the longer reach of the front kick.

- Lead Hand and Lead Foot vs. Lead Hand and Lead Foot: Now the situation is equal, as each student may employ the front hand and front foot for striking. Each student will stay farther away from the other to avoid being kicked. While you will have more options for striking, you will have to guard against strikes that your partner throws at various levels.

- Lead Foot vs. Lead Foot: This drill isolates the front leg tool of each student for development. Because you are limited to kicking with the front leg, you can concentrate on practicing the various lead kicks against your partner and focus on defending against lead leg attacks.

- Lead Foot vs. Lead Hand and Lead Foot: In this drill one student can employ only one tool, the lead foot, while the other student is allowed to use both the lead hand and the lead foot for striking. Therefore, one student only has to be concerned with defending against lead leg attacks, while the other student has to guard against both lead hand and lead foot attacks.

- Lead Foot vs. Lead Hand and Rear Hand: In this drill one student can only use the lead foot to attack. However, he or she has to guard against

Figure 21-2: Lead foot vs. lead hand and rear hand sparring—lead side kick to knee counter against rear cross

lead hand and rear hand attacks. In this position, you will try to take advantage of the longer reach of your front leg, while your partner will try to utilize both hands for striking (see Figure 21-2). When it is your turn to take the other position, you will have to maintain a farther distance against your partner's lead leg and will have to learn how to close the distance in order to strike with your hands.

- Lead Hand and Rear Hand vs. Lead Hand and Rear Hand: This drill allows each student to employ both hands for striking. It will be similar to a Western boxing match in that regard. You will be able to utilize the full range of options available for both hands and not have to worry about being kicked.

> "The best way to learn how to swim is to actually get into the water and swim; the best way to learn Jeet Kune Do is to spar. Only in free sparring can a practitioner begin to learn broken rhythm and the exact timing and correct judgment of distance." (Lee 1997, p. 25)

There are many more drills like these that isolate certain tools for special emphasis. In addition to these you can practice certain drills that stress specific defensive or counteroffensive skills. For instance, you can train on the different counters to the jab to cross combinations that were discussed in the chapter on counterattacks. However, you will do so wearing your sparring equipment against a partner who will be throwing the punches at anywhere from slow speed to full speed. You can work on the various counters to lead side kicks or hook kicks that were also covered in the chapter on counterattacks, but now you will be wearing body armor so that your partner can execute the kicks with power.

You can practice drills that isolate and develop your trapping skills against a live, resisting opponent. These drills will be very challenging as you learn to trap with the boxing gloves on. You should then take it to the next level by working on closing the distance into trapping or by flowing into trapping from kickboxing.

Types of Opponents

When you attack in sparring, you may find that your partners will predominantly react in certain predictable ways. Some will usually open the distance to run away from your attacks. Others will utilize distance to counter your attacks. There are some who will guard and parry at a distance, while others will guard and parry prior to crashing in. Then there are those who will generally press forward.

As you spar, you will learn to recognize these different types of opponents. You will have to discover, through experience, which of the five ways of attack tend to be most successful against each of these types. You will also learn which ones will not work, and why. At the same time you can make it more difficult for your opponents to deal with you by varying your own responses to their attacks. For instance, instead of always evading by opening the distance, you can sometimes parry and crash in. In this way you make yourself less predictable and harder to hit.

Typically students begin to drop out of class when they start to spar hard. They move too quickly into freestyle sparring before they are ready. To ease their way into freestyle sparring, students should first work on sparring drills, which limit the weapons that can be used. That way, students do not feel as overwhelmed.

As he developed his art of Jeet Kune Do, Bruce Lee recognized the importance of sparring with equipment in order to simulate the dynamics of a real fight. The emphasis on sparring distinguished his approach to training from that of other arts that were widely practiced at the time. Sparring continues to play an important role in the development of Jeet Kune Do students today because it allows them to test their skills against a resisting opponent and to experiment with different approaches. Sparring illuminates the true character of each student and, by revealing flaws and weaknesses, shows each student the direction in which he or she needs to go to improve.

part 6
advancing
in jeet kune do

G ROWTH AND PROGRESS in any endeavor, and in Jeet Kune Do in particular, normally does not happen in a nonchalant, haphazard manner. In order to improve in your understanding of the art and your ability to utilize its elements, you should have goals and a plan to achieve them. The next chapter will consider the role of goal setting in Jeet Kune Do training and look at how to set up a training program to meet goals.

Most martial arts systems have a progression through which students move as they advance from a basic to a more complex and sophisticated understanding of the material. We will look at how Jeet Kune Do advancement is set up and how students receive recognition for their progress.

Some Jeet Kune Do students have an interest in testing their skills against other martial artists. With this in mind, the benefits and drawbacks of participating in competitions and tournaments will be considered. Finally, we will also look at how taking part in demonstrations can be a useful way for Jeet Kune Do students to grow in the art.

chapter 22

establishing goals and a training program

ALTHOUGH STUDENTS OF JEET KUNE DO study common principles, techniques, and methods, training is still largely an individual matter. It is up to each individual, in conjunction with the instructor, to establish goals and an appropriate training program to achieve those goals. For instance, many students are attracted to Jeet Kune Do because of its practical, no-nonsense approach to self-defense for the streets. So, surviving an assault is usually an important and worthwhile goal.

However, street survival is usually not the only goal of a martial arts student. Otherwise, such an individual could merely carry a firearm or a knife for self-protection. Typically, a student interested in martial arts training wants to pursue other goals as well. For example, you may want to improve your overall fitness and raise your self-confidence. Therefore, as a student of Jeet Kune Do, you should carefully consider your needs and ensure that your program will help to satisfy those needs.

Setting Goals

Establishing an appropriate training program requires you to identify goals that you want to achieve. Therefore, your first task is to decide on your own goals. Some potential areas that you may want to consider for goal setting include physical, mental, emotional, and spiritual goals. We will examine each of these areas below.

Physical Goals

This is the area that most students of Jeet Kune Do are, at least initially, primarily interested in improving. Often, through watching some of Bruce Lee's films or reading about his martial art in books or magazines, prospective students become convinced that they can become good fighters if they train in Jeet Kune Do. Becoming a good fighter, however, requires more than just learning the physical techniques of the art. You must also improve certain of your own attributes in order to make the art work for you.

Strengthening power is one goal that should definitely be high on a Jeet Kune Do student's list. Without power supporting your techniques, you will not be able

> A basic fitness program that was recorded in Lee's notes consisted of the following: (1) alternate splits, (2) push-up, (3) run in place, (4) shoulder circling, (5) high kicks, (6) deep knee bends, (7) side kick raises, (8) sit-up (twist), (9) waist twisting, (10) leg raises, and (11) forward bends.

to hurt or to stop your opponent. The principle of intercepting will have little meaning because your stop-hit or stop-kick will fail to halt your opponent.

Speed is another attribute that a student should improve. There are two primary types of speed that you should develop: movement speed and reaction speed. Power depends largely upon cultivation of movement speed, which refers to how quickly you can execute a technique. Reaction speed refers to the amount of time it takes for your brain to recognize an event—such as a punch coming at you or an opening in your opponent's defenses—and to send the right signals to your body to respond appropriately.

Another attribute that you should improve is flexibility. This refers to the elasticity of your muscles—that is, how far you can stretch them. A person whose legs are flexible has a greater range in kicking heights, for example, than an individual whose leg muscles are stiff. Therefore, the more flexible you are, the more target areas you can reach with your kicks. It is also harder for your opponent to defend against your kick if he or she has to worry about defending targets at various heights.

Coordination and dexterity are additional physical attributes that a Jeet Kune Do student should develop. Coordination has to do with synchronizing your movements so that they work together, while dexterity refers to moving with ease and skill. Although some people seem to be blessed with more coordination and dexterity than others, everyone can take steps to improve these attributes. Jeet Kune Do students who can make various movements operate in an adept manner will move more economically and smoothly.

Enhanced health and fitness are two important physical goals for which the Jeet Kune Do student should strive. These affect not only your performance in fighting, but also other areas of your life as well. If you possess good health and a high level of fitness, you will improve your skills more rapidly than a person in poor health and low level of fitness. You will be able to train longer, more often, and more intensely. The physical training involved in Jeet Kune Do helps to relieve and reduce stress, which in turn contributes to better health and fitness.

Mental Goals

Another important area in which you should set goals has to do with the mind. Traditionally, martial arts have been credited with enhancing a person's mental capacity in addition to physical ability. Jeet Kune Do training should be geared toward improving your mind as well as your body.

One aspect of mental health that is directly related to the idea of self-defense is developing greater awareness of yourself and your environment. In fighting you need to be aware of your opponent's position, actions, and intentions. In addition, you should be alert to your own body position, movement, and intention, relative to your opponent. You also need to recognize your surroundings, such as walls or avenues of escape. All these elements influence decisions that you will make regarding your ability to defend yourself effectively.

You will also want to improve your perception of events. For example, you should develop your capacity to recognize when your opponent is preparing to strike, so that you can respond appropriately and in a timely fashion. Moreover, you ought to strengthen your ability to recognize when your opponent may be ripe for a counterattack—when his attention is diverted, for example, or when she relaxes her guard.

Enhanced self-esteem, self-image, and self-confidence are all worthy goals that you should strive for in your training. Learning and mastering various skills should affirm that you are a person of value who has been blessed with talent and ability. When you successfully achieve something in Jeet Kune Do, you naturally feel good about yourself, which strengthens your sense of self.

Two additional goals that the Jeet Kune Do student should consider are better balance and harmony. Training in martial arts can help you focus your thinking and center yourself. It can help relieve the pressure of work, school, and other concerns. Understanding the balance and coordination needed in martial arts can inspire you to seek the same harmony in other areas of your life.

Emotional Goals

Fights tend to result from a heightening of people's negative emotions. The act of fighting itself also intensifies the emotions that the combatants feel. When they are allowed free rein and remain unchecked, such emotions can impair your ability to think clearly and to fight effectively. However, when you manage them properly, you can channel your feelings so that your fighting contains, in Bruce Lee's words, "emotional content."

> "You see, the kicks and punches are weapons not necessarily aimed toward invading opponents. These tools can be aimed at our fears, frustrations, and all that. Martial art can help in your process toward growth." (Lee 1997, p. 30)

Therefore, an important goal for you, as a Jeet Kune Do student, is to learn to manage your emotions in fighting so that you stay cool under pressure. You should strive to control fear, anxiety, and anger when facing an opponent. You need to deal with the inevitable adrenaline rush that results from the fight or flight response to the perception of danger.

Learning to get along and cooperating with others is another important goal in the emotional area. Jeet Kune Do training helps because you are forced to work with other people who are often strangers, at least in the beginning. Because you are all striving together to improve and to grow, you look out for the others' interests, not only your own. You also forge a strong bond based on mutual interests.

To help you reach your goals, find people who will work with you, guide you, support you, and keep you accountable. Besides your instructor, enlist the help of your fellow students, family, friends, and coworkers to help you maintain progress.

Spiritual Goals

Training in Jeet Kune Do can lead to better understanding of the fragility of life, as you learn how easy it is for someone to cause serious injury, or even death, to another human being. This, in turn, can deepen your appreciation of and respect for the sanctity of human life and the spiritual interconnectedness of all human beings. Moreover, it can strengthen your respect for the Creator of yourself and all men and women. As you strengthen your body physically, your training also forges your mind, heart, and spirit.

Establishing a Training Program

Once you have identified specific goals that you wish to attain, you can design a training program that will help you reach those goals. Such a program is, by necessity, highly individualized because your combination of goals is unique to you. Also, it must take into account factors such as your age, schedule, level of fitness, and preferences.

- Classes/Private Sessions: First, you should set up a schedule for your technique training. This should consist of the classes or private sessions that you will attend on a regular basis. If you are attending a school, you will probably have classes that are set on certain days and times. You should ensure that you can attend these classes when scheduled, so that you can train regularly. If you are studying privately with an instructor, you should select the days and times that you can make on a regular basis. Consistency in training is important in order to maintain steady progress and growth in your knowledge and skills.

- Strength Training: To improve your power and your overall health and fitness, you may wish to establish a strength-training program. There are numerous ways to do this. One way, of course, is to join a gym or fitness club where you can have access to weight-lifting and strength-training equipment. Another way is to purchase equipment that you can use at home. The latter option is more convenient, of course, but you must have space to store the equipment when not in use.

- Cardiovascular Training: To improve your conditioning and endurance, you should develop a program for cardiovascular work. This can involve any type of activity that challenges you aerobically, including jogging, running, hiking, aerobics, swimming, cycling, and rollerblading. It is recommended that you do your strength and weight training and your aerobic training on alternate days. For instance, you can lift weights on Mondays, Wednesdays, and Fridays and jog on Tuesdays, Thursdays, and Saturdays. Having days off in-between weight-lifting sessions gives your muscles a chance to heal and to grow.

- Cross-Training: Participating in other sports can also provide benefits that will affect your martial arts training. Cycling can improve your conditioning and endurance. Swimming works many of your muscles and also helps with conditioning. Cross-country skiing strengthens your conditioning as well. Basketball enhances your conditioning and footwork, while dance helps with balance and footwork.

- Heavy Bag/Speed Bag/Top and Bottom Bag: You can develop power in your kicks and punches by practicing them on a heavy bag—large containers made of leather or canvas and filled with fabric, which can withstand the hardest strikes. Speed bags—small, air-filled bags that are hung at head level—enable you to work on your hand-eye coordination as well as improve the speed of your punches. The top and bottom bag is a small ball that is tethered to the ceiling and the ground with rope; it helps in proper alignment of your punches and allows you to practice your defenses, such as slipping and ducking.

> Identifying goals and ways to reach them requires an honest evaluation of one's strengths and weaknesses. This can be particularly intimidating for students who have already trained for years in martial arts. They must overcome their pride to realize that there are gaps in their training that must be addressed.

- Practice Sessions: It can be very beneficial to meet on a regular basis with one or more students to practice material that has been taught. These sessions will reinforce the learning of the material and can deepen your understanding of it. Also, it is a great way to develop friendships with others.
- Sparring: Whether in class or in practice sessions, regular sparring can help you to improve your coordination, timing, and distance. From an emotional standpoint frequent sparring sessions will help you to become accustomed to dealing with being hit. Through sparring you learn to control your anger and fear and to deal with situations in a more relaxed, even-tempered way.

Training without purpose is a waste of energy and effort. To obtain the most from your training, you need to identify your goals and establish a training program that will help you attain those goals. Work together with your instructor and other students so that they can assist you in remaining on track.

chapter 23

phase advancement

UNLIKE MANY traditional martial arts systems, Jeet Kune Do has never had a formal belt ranking system. Bruce Lee did not believe in belts to denote one's rank or ability and, therefore, did not employ them. However, in the 1960s, when he started the third and final Jun Fan Gung Fu Institute in Los Angeles, he did establish a rudimentary ranking structure and awarded rank via certificates. Dan Inosanto, who served as Lee's assistant instructor at the Institute, was given a third rank in Jeet Kune Do. Most students who trained for a sufficient period of time were awarded a first rank. Not long after, however, Lee stopped issuing certificates of rank.

*G*enerally speaking, most individuals who study Jeet Kune Do do so in order gain knowledge and improve skills. They are more concerned with growing and developing than with gaining any type of formal rank or recognition.

It was not until after Lee's passing that Inosanto, then the recognized head of Jeet Kune Do, created a new ranking structure. When he began the Filipino Kali Academy in 1974, he instituted a four-level phase system that denoted one's level of training in the art. A student had to complete Phases 1, 2, 3, and 4 before becoming eligible for induction into what was then a single Jeet Kune Do class. Later on, Inosanto and Taky Kimura, Lee's assistant instructor at the Seattle Jun Fan Gung Fu Institute, developed a modified ranking structure consisting of eight levels, with Bruce Lee at level eight.

Over the years, as more students have become instructors and established schools or training programs, they have instituted their own ranking structures. These structures vary widely in the ways that they recognize student advancement. These range from virtually no rank given at all to multilevels and sublevels of rank. Consequently, there is no single, uniform ranking structure that is consistently used by all Jeet Kune Do instructors.

However, there are those who still adhere to a four-phase structure that resembles the type used by Inosanto in the 1970s and 1980s, a form that he continues to use in his Academy today. This is probably the closest to a widely recognized system of advancement that exists in Jeet Kune Do.

Generally speaking, each of these four phases can vary in the amount of time required to complete it. Students who train two times a week on a regular basis can probably expect to spend about nine months to a year or more in each phase, depending upon their progress.

> It is interesting to note that, although many Jeet Kune Do instructors use some type of ranking or certification system, Lee himself never possessed a belt, sash, or rank in any system, including Wing Chun. He also never referred to himself as a "master" or "grandmaster," but only as a "sifu" or "teacher."

Phase 1 typically focuses on establishing a good foundation in footwork and in tool development—that is, learning how to properly kick and punch. Students learn how to correctly execute the lead hand and rear hand strikes, as well as lead and rear kicks. They work on proper body mechanics and moving from the bai-jong stance. Training is usually limited to use of resistance equipment, such as focus mitts and kicking shields. Basic trapping hands, such as pak sao and lop sao, may be studied in this phase as well.

Phase 2 usually builds upon this foundation by having students work on refining the tools by making the movements more economical. Students may be introduced to some or all of the five ways of attack. Often they will start learning some of the various defenses to an opponent's attack. The majority of the training will still involve the use of resistance equipment. Students may also learn more of the trapping hands, including compound traps. Depending upon the instructor, students may take start to take part in limited sparring drills.

> The length of time required to become an instructor in Jeet Kune Do can vary greatly. Most instructors generally require at least a few years of regular, consistent training. A few will certify students after they complete a concentrated block of training. Still others will not certify, even if a student has spent many years in training.

In Phase 3 students continue to work on the five ways of attack. They are also likely to explore defenses, such as bob and weave, slipping, and evasion, in depth. Students also typically study ways to counterattack at this point. Progressive sparring plays a more prominent role at this stage, as students seek to apply their knowledge in real time. Energy and sensitivity drills for trapping may also be practiced. Grappling may be introduced at this stage as well.

Finally, in Phase 4 students integrate the knowledge that they have learned in the previous phases. They are expected to have a working knowledge of all the various kicks, punches, close-quarters strikes, and traps. They develop the ability to flow easily from range to range, executing the appropriate tools in the right situations. They concentrate more on tactical elements such as distance, timing, and rhythm. They spar in the various ranges with more intensity, wearing protective equipment. By this time, they should have an appreciation for the philosophy and principles of Jeet Kune Do and be able to assist in teaching if called upon to do so.

It is important to understand that, while no uniform ranking system is utilized throughout the Jeet Kune Do community, there is still a definite progression to training. You must begin by establishing a firm foundation in the fundamentals of the art before you can master the more complex elements of attack, defense, counterattack, distance, and timing, to name a few. As you gain proficiency in the various aspects of Jeet Kune Do, you will grow in your sophistication and working knowledge of the art. This applies whether you are one of many in a school or whether you train privately. In this way you will be able to grow into a well-rounded fighter, able to handle a multitude of situations with confidence.

Many schools and teachers have various levels of instructorship in Jeet Kune Do. Typically, an advanced student starts as an apprentice instructor. After a period of time in that category, he or she can be promoted to associate instructor. A few go on to become full instructors. Finally, a select number move on to senior instructor level.

competitions and demonstrations

Competitions

IN THE EARLY YEARS of Jeet Kune Do's development, students were generally not encouraged to take part in organized competitions. Many of the tournaments that took place at the time had rules that greatly limited the types of techniques that participants could use. Quite popular during this period were the "point-karate" style gatherings, in which players deliberately refrained from employing full power in their strikes so as not to hurt their opponents. Competitors were awarded points for executing techniques at certain targets that could have caused damage if they actually landed.

When asked why Bruce Lee never competed, Dan Inosanto, his student, used a beauty contest analogy. A beautiful girl does not have to enter a beauty contest to prove that she is beautiful. Likewise, Lee did not have to enter competitions to prove he could fight.

Needless to say, with his emphasis on practical, realistic street fighting, Bruce Lee did not look favorably on these types of competitions. Instead, he believed that sparring, with protective equipment, represented the ultimate test of one's fighting skills. At both the Oakland and Los Angeles Jun Fan Gung Fu Institutes, students regularly took part in sparring drills that developed their sense of timing, distance, and rhythm. Lee himself occasionally sparred with some of his students, although for him it was more play than actual sparring.

The one type of contest that Lee did appreciate was the full-contact karate tournament. These types of tournaments provide more realistic fighting dynamics than the point-karate ones. Lee respected and befriended a number of the top competitors of the time. The most celebrated of them, Joe Lewis, trained with Lee and incorporated some of Lee's theories of fighting, such as the five ways of attack, into his tournament fighting style. Armed with the knowledge that he gained from Lee, he managed to become what many consider to be the greatest full-contact karate champion of all time. Lewis has publicly given credit to Lee for his contributions to his accomplishments in the ring.

Today, the competition scene has changed dramatically from Lee's day. Organized tournaments for practitioners of traditional arts, such as karate and taekwondo, continue to attract students of those systems. In recent years, other types of contests have also gained in popularity. These include Muay Thai and kickboxing tournaments, grappling competitions, especially in Brazilian jujitsu, and mixed martial arts events that feature stand-up and ground fighting styles.

However, there is still no organized competition specifically geared for Jeet Kune Do students. It seems that the Jeet Kune Do community at-large has no burning desire to establish or operate its own events for students of Lee's art. This is probably due, in large part, to the fact that many instructors already include sparring as part of the training that their students must undergo. Many of these students have ample opportunities within their own training to explore combat against a live opponent. Because the fighting skills of students are tested through sparring, many see no need to test their skills in a structured, competitive setting.

Nevertheless, more Jeet Kune Do students these days are interested in participating in organized competitions, wanting to test their skills against outside players. Those that do take part, however, typically fight with the specific arts that are emphasized in these competitions, rather than using Jeet Kune Do. For example, some have extensively studied grappling arts, such as Brazilian jujitsu and shoot wrestling, and engage in contests in which they can showcase their skills in these arts. Others compete in mixed martial arts gatherings. Indeed, the mixed martial arts events are probably the closest to what a Jeet Kune Do competition might look like, because they allow the different kicking, punching, elbowing, kneeing, and grappling tools.

One of the limitations of these types of events, though, is that they are specifically sporting events. As such, they typically do not allow kicks and shots to the groin, eye jabs and eye pokes, or kicks to the knee or shin. These techniques are a mainstay of the Jeet Kune Do practitioner's arsenal. Therefore, the Jeet Kune Do fighter who participates in these competitions cannot use the full range of tools and techniques that would be available in a street fight.

Nevertheless, despite these restrictions, organized competitions can provide Jeet Kune Do students with an excellent opportunity to grow and develop as fighters. Particularly in mixed martial arts events, Jeet Kune Do students can employ many of the various tools at the different ranges. They can also practice assorted tactical elements, such as timing, distance, and rhythm. Practitioners of Lee's art can also use the five ways of attack, as well as the various defenses and counterattacks. In addition, competing in these events allows students to learn to manage their emotions, as they are forced to deal with opponents who are attacking them with speed and power. Because their opponents will more than likely be strangers, they have to learn how to quickly assess their strengths and weaknesses. In short, competitions can be a useful laboratory in which to experiment with the different aspects of Jeet Kune Do. Regardless of whether students win or lose, they can benefit from the experience gained from competing in these events.

Demonstrations

Unlike competitions, demonstrations have been a part of Jeet Kune Do from the beginning. During his early years in the United States, Bruce Lee gave demonstrations of what was, at that time, the little-known art of Chinese gung fu. Later, on separate occasions he demonstrated his martial arts at Ed Parker's Long Beach International Karate Tournament. In fact, a Hollywood producer managed to view a film of one of these demonstrations, which eventually led to the casting of Lee in the role of Kato in the *Green Hornet* television series. Many in the martial arts community witnessed the speed, power, and deceptiveness of Jeet Kune Do as Lee sparred, showed how he closed the distance, and exhibited the one-inch punch.

Over the years Dan Inosanto, who basically headed the Jeet Kune Do clan

When putting on a demonstration of Jeet Kune Do, keep in mind that a large audience cannot see the subtleties of the art. So it is probably wise to stay away from trapping or locks. Instead, focus on areas that require larger, more visible movements, such as kickboxing or grappling, which are also more exciting to watch.

After staying out of the limelight for many years, some of Lee's students have become more willing to publicly demonstrate their knowledge of Lee's art. They have done so at seminars sponsored by the Bruce Lee Educational Foundation and, more recently, at an inaugural Bruce Lee Convention in Southern California.

after Lee passed away, often organized demonstrations with his students. These exhibitions of Lee's art, as well as Filipino Kali-Escrima, took place at different public events, such as Asian heritage festivals. Members of the public had a rare opportunity to be exposed to certain selected aspects of Jeet Kune Do at these demonstrations. Other Jeet Kune Do instructors have continued the tradition of giving public displays of Lee's art to the community.

Demonstrations are a good way for a Jeet Kune Do instructor to attract potential students who can see Lee's art firsthand. There are, of course, no hard and fast rules as to how to put on a demonstration. A given demonstration might showcase one or more aspects of Jeet Kune Do, such as kicking, punching, trapping, and grappling. Multiple-attack scenarios might be played out during these exhibitions. Focus mitt drills and sparring, which are enjoyable to watch, are training methods that can be included in the demonstrations.

The idea is for the demonstration to entertain as well as to educate. Explanations should be kept simple and not highly technical. The essence of the technique should be emphasized, rather than the small details. Preparing to take part in the demonstrations can inspire students to focus on refining their movements and improving their speed and power. Practicing and training for a demonstration helps them to concentrate their energy and effort toward an identifiable objective. It can help improve their self-confidence, as they are required to show their skills in public before strangers. Those who speak during the demonstration will undoubtedly strengthen their public speaking skills. Most of all, though, students will find the experience educational and enjoyable.

Because they have specific objectives, competitions and demonstrations can give Jeet Kune Do students focus in their training. On the one hand, competitions can provide students with an opportunity to test their skills in a non-school setting against martial artists of other styles. This can be a tremendous learning experience as students discover what does and does not work for them in a high-pressure environment.

Demonstrations, on the other hand, can give students a chance to display their knowledge and skill in a way that educates the public about the effectiveness of Jeet Kune Do. Students can gain confidence in themselves as they show their abilities at these exhibitions. They can contribute, in a meaningful way, to the perpetuation of Lee's art as a viable approach to self-defense and fighting for today's world.

One of the more renowned Jeet Kune Do practitioners to compete in major events is Erik Paulson. He has been a shoot fighting champion in Japan and recently participated in a grappling competition. He also took part in an early grappling tournament where his stated style was "Jun Fan," in homage to Bruce Lee's approach to martial arts.

Books

Balicki, Ron, with Dr. Steven Gold. *Jeet Kune Do: Principles of a Complete Fighter*. Manchester, England: Health 'N' Life Publishing, 2001.

Cheung, William, and Ted Wong. *Wing Chun Kung Fu/Jeet Kune Do: A Comparison*, Vol. 1. Valencia: Black Belt Communications, 1990.

Clouse, Robert. *Bruce Lee: The Biography*. Burbank: Unique Publications, 1989.

Davis, Lamar II. *Jun Fan/Jeet Kune Do: Scientific Streetfighting*. Manchester, England: Health 'N' Life Publishing, 2001.

DeMile, James W. *Bruce Lee's 1 and 3 Inch Power Punch*. Burbank: Unique Publications, 1992.

Fraguas, Jose M. *Jeet Kune Do Conversations*. Burbank: Unique Publications, 2002.

Glover, Jesse. *Bruce Lee Between Wing Chun and Jeet Kune Do*. Seattle, Washington: Glover Publications, 1976.

——. *Bruce Lee's Non-Classical Gung Fu*. Seattle, Washington: Glover Publications, 1978.

Hartsell, Larry. *Jeet Kune Do: Conditioning and Grappling Methods*. Manchester, England: Health 'N' Life Publishing, 2002.

——. *Jeet Kune Do: Entering to Trapping to Grappling*. Burbank: Unique Publications, 1989.

——. *Jeet Kune Do: Hardcore Training & Strategies Guide*. Manchester, England: Health 'N' Life Publishing, 2002.

Hartsell, Larry, and Tim Tackett. *Jeet Kune Do: Counterattack! Grappling Counters and Reversals*. Burbank: Unique Publications, 1987.

Inosanto, Dan. *Absorb What Is Useful* (Jeet Kune Do Guidebook, Vol. 2). Burbank: Unique Publications, 1982.

——. *Jeet Kune Do: The Art and Philosophy of Bruce Lee.* Los Angeles: Know Now Publishing Co., 1994.

Kent, Chris. *Jeet Kune Do: From A to Z*, Vol. 1. Burbank: Unique Publications, 2000.

——. *Jeet Kune Do: From A to Z*, Vol. 2. Burbank: Unique Publications, 2001.

Kent, Chris, and Tim Tackett. *Jeet Kune Do Kickboxing.* Burbank: Unique Publications, 1989.

——. *Jun Fan/Jeet Kune Do: The Textbook.* Burbank: Unique Publications, 1989.

Lee, Bruce. *Tao of Jeet Kune Do.* Valencia: Black Belt Communications, 1993.

Lee, Bruce, and John Little, ed. *The Art of Expressing the Human Body* (The Bruce Lee Library, Vol. 4). Boston: Tuttle Publishing, 1998.

——. *Jeet Kune Do: Bruce Lee's Commentaries on the Martial Way* (The Bruce Lee Library, Vol. 3). Boston: Tuttle Publishing, 1997.

——. *The Tao of Gung Fu: A Study in the Way of Chinese Martial Art* (The Bruce Lee Library, Vol. 2). Boston: Tuttle Publishing, 1997.

Lee, Bruce, and Mitoshi Uyehara. *Bruce Lee's Fighting Method, Vol. 1: Self-Defense Techniques.* Valencia: Black Belt Communications, 1988.

——. *Bruce Lee's Fighting Method, Vol. 2: Basic Training.* Valencia: Black Belt Communications, 1988.

——. *Bruce Lee's Fighting Method, Vol. 3: Skill in Techniques.* Valencia: Black Belt Communications, 1988.

——. *Bruce Lee's Fighting Method, Vol. 4: Advanced Techniques.* Valencia: Black Belt Communications, 1989.

Lee, Linda. *The Bruce Lee Story.* Valencia: Black Belt Communications, 1989.

Little, John. *Bruce Lee: A Warrior's Journey.* Chicago: McGraw Hill/Contemporary Books, 2001.

Seaman, Kevin. *Jun Fan Gung Fu: Seeking the Path of Jeet Kune Do.* Manchester, England: Health 'N' Life Publishing, 2001.

Vunak, Paul. *Jeet Kune Do: Its Concepts and Philosophies.* Burbank: Unique Publications, 1994.

Videos

Bustillo, Richard and Ted Wong. *Bruce Lee's Fighting Method: Basic Training & Self Defense Techniques*. Valencia: Black Belt Magazine Video, 1999.

Dixon, Barry. *Combat Jeet Kune Do*. Burbank: Unique Publications Video.
    Vol. 1: "SDA – Simple Direct Attack"
    Vol. 2: "ABC – Attack by Combination"
    Vol. 3: "Counterattack"
    Vol. 4: "JKD Conditioning Skills"

Grody, Steve. *Jun Fan/Jeet Kune Do Trapping and Sectoring Skills*. Burbank: Unique Publications Video (four volumes).

Inosanto, Dan. *The Definitive Dan Inosanto Collection*. Los Angeles: Inosanto Academy of Martial Arts. 2000.
    Vol. I: "Jun Fan Gung Fu/JKD Kickboxing"
    Vol. II: "Jun Fan Gung Fu/JKD Trapping"
    Vol. III: "Jun Fan Gung Fu/JKD Grappling"

Kent, Chris. *Dynamic Jeet Kune Do*. Los Angeles: Health for Life, 1996.
    Vol. 1: "Building a Strong Foundation"
    Vol. 2: "Think Hit!"
    Vol. 3: "Adapt Like a Shadow: Respond Like an Echo"
    Vol. 4: "Putting It All Together"

Kent, Chris. *Jeet Kune Do: From A to Z*. Burbank: Unique Publications Video, 2000.
    Vol. 1: "Mastering the Basics"
    Vol. 2: "Jeet Kune Do Strikes"
    Vol. 3: "Scientific Streetfighting"
    Vol. 4: "Advanced Strategies"
    Vol. 5: "Know the Moment"

Poteet, Jerry. *Jeet Kune Do*. Los Angeles: Tortoise Video, 1990.
    Vol. 1: "Foundation"
    Vol. 2: "Dynamics of Hitting & Kicking"
    Vol. 3: "Trapping: The Nucleus of JKD"
    Vol. 4: "The 5 Ways of Attack"
    Vol. 5: "Equipment & Supplemental Training"
    Vol. 6: "For Women & Children"

Poteet, Jerry. *Jeet Kune Do*. Sherman Oaks: Silver Fox Videos, 2000/2002.
Series 2, Tape 1: "Low Line Attacks," 2002.
Series 2, Tape 2: "Explosive Wooden Dummy Training," 2000.

Strong, Patrick. *Bruce Lee*. Los Angeles: Rising Sun Video Productions, 2000–2001.
Tape 1: "The Lord of Speed," 2001.
Tape 2: "The Lord of Shock," 2001.
Tape 3: "The Lord of Power," 2001.
Tape 4: "Bruce Lee's Inner Game," 2000.

Tucci, Rick. Jeet *Kune Do*. New York: ESPY-TV.
Vol. 1: "Introduction to Jun Fan"
Vol. 2: "Jun Fan Trapping"
Vol. 3: "Jun Fan Kickboxing to Trapping—Blending the Ranges of JKD"
Vol. 4: "Jun Fan Kickboxing to Locking"

Vunak, Paul. *Mastering Jeet Kune Do Concepts & Filipino Martial Arts*. San Clemente: Panther Productions, 1985.
Vol. 1: "Jun Fan Kickboxing"
Vol. 2: "Jun Fan Kickboxing"
Vol. 3: "Trapping"
Vol. 4: "Wing Chun Dummy Training"

Periodicals

Black Belt Magazine. P.O. Box 420235, Palm Coast, Florida 32142-0235.
www.blackbeltmag.com

Inside Kung Fu. CFW Enterprises, Inc., 4201 Vanowen Place, Burbank, California 91505. www.cfwenterprises.com

Kung Fu/Qigong. Pacific Rim Publishing, 40748 Encyclopedia Circle, Fremont, California 94538. www.kungfumagazine.com

Martial Arts Illustrated. Martial Arts Limited, Revenue Chambers, St. Peters Street, Huddersfield HD1 1DL, UK.

about the author

David Cheng is the Director and Chief Instructor of Combative Martial Arts Systems, based in the Los Angeles area. He is one of only about a dozen individuals in the entire world to be certified as a Full Instructor in Jeet Kune Do and Filipino Kali-Escrima under Chris Kent, world-renowned teacher and author of numerous books on Jeet Kune Do training and philosophy. He teaches regular group classes and private sessions in the art of Jeet Kune Do, as well as in Filipino Kali-Escrima. Sifu Cheng has taught self-defense courses at local community adult programs and for other organizations. He is also a founder and codirector of the inaugural Jeet Kune Do Leadership Training Workshop.

Sifu Cheng is an official representative of the Chris Kent Jeet Kune Do/Kali-Escrima Association. He has also participated in the videotape series *Jeet Kune Do: From A to Z* and in the companion book series. Sifu Cheng has written and been featured in many articles on Jeet Kune Do and Filipino Kali-Escrima for *Inside Kung Fu*, *Martial Arts Legends*, *Jeet Kune Do Guide*, *Bruce Lee's JKD Legacy*, *Martial Arts Superstars*, and other publications.

For information on instruction, consultation, workshops, seminars, and instructor certification programs, contact Sifu Cheng at one of the following addresses:

Combative Martial Arts Systems
23706 Crenshaw Boulevard
Suite 104
Torrance, California 90505

E-mail: kalijeetkunedo@yahoo.com
www.geocities.com/kalijeetkunedo